"The authors cover a vital but often poorly-understood issue in the public sector. Their book covers considerable ground, taking the reader from the basics of logistics and transport through to complex issues and current challenges such as technology and sustainability. Throughout, the writing is clear, insightful and well referenced, with useful and relevant case studies."

Peter Smith, *Chartered Institute of Procurement and Supply past president, ex-chief procurement officer and business author*

MANAGING LOGISTICS AND TRANSPORTATION IN THE PUBLIC SECTOR

Managing Logistics and Transportation in the Public Sector, Second Edition thoroughly examines the world of transportation as it relates to public procurement, stressing the importance of not only procuring the right goods, materials, and services, but also ensuring their proper delivery to their final destination. Designed to educate the public procurement professional on ways to realize enhanced cost savings, it offers an introduction to the history of transportation, as well as industry terminology and accepted practices. Authors Darin Matthews and Linda Stanley explore recent transportation industry evolutions, including the development of important technologies like package tracing, delivery notification, and drone delivery, and ways to successfully integrate this technology. Sustainability in transportation—including product packaging, material reuse, and reduced emissions for delivery vehicles—is likewise examined. Through the use of case studies and transportation industry resources, *Managing Logistics and Transportation in the Public Sector, Second Edition* offers a complete package for public procurement professionals looking to enhance their knowledge of logistics and transportation, as well as for university courses on transportation, supply chain management, and public procurement.

Darin L. Matthews is the chief procurement officer for California Polytechnic State University, San Luis Obispo. He has over 30 years of procurement and supply management experience in local government, higher education and the private sector. Darin has served as adjunct faculty for University of California, Portland State University, and Florida Atlantic University. His articles on procurement have been featured in *Government Procurement*, *Journal of Public Procurement*, and *International Handbook of Public Procurement*. Darin's books include *Effective Supply Management Performance* (with Dr. Linda Stanley), *Warehousing and Inventory Control* (with Dr. Jerry Giankis), and *Public Procurement* (with Dr. Alexandru Roman).

Linda L. Stanley is an author and retired professor. She was a faculty associate for 14 years at Arizona State University, a visiting professor at Arizona State University West and associate professor and chair of the Management Department at Our Lady of the Lake University in Texas. She has taught logistics, strategic procurement, purchasing and supply management, negotiation, and other supply management topics. Linda has been published extensively in several industry journals, including *Journal of Operations Management, Journal of Supply Chain Management*, and *Journal of Business Logistics*. She also has two other published books, *Process Management, Creating Value along the Supply Chain* (with Joel Wisner), and *Effective Supply Management Performance* (with Darin Matthews).

Cornerstones of Public Procurement

NIGP - The Institute for Public Procurement, USA

Recently Published Books

The Legal Aspects of Public Procurement, Third Edition
Michael Flynn, Kirk W. Buffington and Richard Pennington

Developing and Managing Requests for Proposals in the Public Sector, Third Edition
Ronald King, Theresa Bauccio-Teschlog, Dennis Carney, Joyce Foster and Christine Webber

Managing Logistics and Transportation in the Public Sector, Second Edition
Darin L. Matthews and Linda L. Stanley

MANAGING LOGISTICS AND TRANSPORTATION IN THE PUBLIC SECTOR

Second Edition

DARIN L. MATTHEWS
AND LINDA L. STANLEY

Routledge
Taylor & Francis Group
NEW YORK AND LONDON

Cover image: Getty Images

Second edition published 2023
by Routledge
605 Third Avenue, New York, NY 10158

and by Routledge
4 Park Square, Milton Park, Abingdon, Oxon, OX14 4RN

Routledge is an imprint of the Taylor & Francis Group, an informa business

First edition published by NIGP 2007

Library of Congress Cataloging-in-Publication Data
Names: Stanley, Linda L., author. | Matthews, Darin, author.
Title: Managing logistics and transportation in the public sector / Linda L. Stanley and Darin L. Matthews. Other titles: Logistics and transportation
Identifiers: LCCN 2021062116 (print) | LCCN 2021062117 (ebook) | ISBN 9781032288116 (hardback) | ISBN 9781003298625 (ebook)
Subjects: LCSH: Business logistics. | Government purchasing. | Physical distribution of goods.
Classification: LCC HD38.5 .S7325 2022 (print) | LCC HD38.5 (ebook) | DDC 658.7—dc23/eng/20220314
LC record available at https://lccn.loc.gov/2021062116
LC ebook record available at https://lccn.loc.gov/2021062117

ISBN: 978-1-032-28811-6 (hbk)
ISBN: 978-1-003-29862-5 (ebk)

DOI: 10.4324/9781003298625

Typeset in Adobe Garamond Pro
by Apex CoVantage, LLC

I would first like to thank my spouse, Dana, for her role as my editor, advisor and confidant during this project and many others. This is the fourth collaboration with Dr. Linda Stanley and I believe it to be our best. She is always professional, insightful, and well organized, and frankly the best co-author around. Finally, this book would not be possible without the support and leadership of the team at NIGP: The Institute for Public Procurement.

Darin L Matthews

My heartfelt thanks go to the staff at NIGP who invited me to co-author the second edition of this book. Thanks also go to Darin Matthews, my writing partner, who shared his many years of public procurement experience and made the writing process a smooth one. Many others in the field of public procurement shared their wisdom and provided valuable feedback at the beginning of this process. Lastly, I would like to thank my husband Kim for supporting me throughout the project, who was always loving and supportive.

Linda L. Stanley

Contents

Figures

Chapter 1

Logistics and Transportation—Overview

Introduction

The management of logistics and transportation decisions is frequently an overlooked opportunity to improve governmental and not-for-profit operations and save money. Many public procurement professionals are unfamiliar with the costs of transportation and unaware of potential opportunities for savings. Traditionally, the procurement and management of transportation services have been relegated to the supplier, which provides a "laid-down price" or "landed cost"—the cost of transportation rolled into the price of purchased goods.

However, there are a number of reasons why public procurement professionals should have a better understanding of transportation decisions. First, there is a cost attached when Procurement delegates this decision to the supplier. For example, suppliers often add a fixed amount for transportation based on the purchase price, which is higher than the actual amount charged by the transportation provider. Without a clear understanding of the transportation industry, the procurement professional trusts the supplier to charge fairly for this service. The supplier should, at a minimum, disclose the transportation charges. This could be done by requiring free on board (FOB) destination in

DOI: 10.4324/9781003298625-1

the contract, in which transportation charges are paid by the shipper. To take it a step further, Procurement should negotiate directly with a few respected transportation providers and consolidate shipments, resulting in significant cost savings.

Second, consolidation and control translate into a stronger position with the transportation provider, resulting in better service. Specific needs—such as special drop-off points, deliveries during certain operating hours or shipments on specific pallet sizes—are now possible. If left to the supplier, service needs may not be met. Also, some carriers operate as logistics service companies and will integrate their expertise with that of their customers (Anonymous, 2016a). Finally, as public procurement moves toward more contract negotiation, understanding the transportation portion of the contract is critical. Rather than focusing on price alone, government entities can realize the value of evaluating the *total cost* of procuring goods, which could include transportation costs, carrying costs, repair and maintenance costs, and disposal costs, among others. Consideration of these costs is increasingly a factor in contract negotiations today. More on negotiating the contract can be found in Chapter 5.

Thus, savings opportunities and better service options can be realized by paying closer attention to the details of the transportation decision, whether directly arranged by the procurement professional or managed by a supplier. The components of procuring transportation services include:

- evaluating the prices of various transportation services;
- determining the effect of a particular transportation service on operations; and
- evaluating the effect of transit times, carrier dependability, and safe delivery on inventory levels, selection of modes, carriers, and service options.

(Johnson, 2020)

Other important decisions include:

- looking for opportunities to reduce transportation and inventory carrying costs;
- expediting and tracing shipments; and
- auditing and processing claims for damaged goods or over/underpayments.

The selection of a transportation system is a specialized form of procurement in which services are purchased to provide a link between manufacturing sites, warehouses, distribution centers, or office sites. More on this topic can be found in Chapter 3.

This chapter will begin with an introduction to some commonly used logistics terms. A short history of logistics and transportation is provided, followed by some statistics on logistical expenditures in the United States. Next, the chapter discusses where logistics fits into an entity's planning process. Lastly, some current trends and challenges for the industry are described.

Common Transportation and Logistics Terms

Transportation is "the physical movement of goods and people between points" (Wood & Johnson, 1995, p. 4). Procured goods may include new materials brought into a production process or finished goods shipped to the customer. The *consignee* is the party—usually the buyer—that receives the goods sent by the *consignor*, usually the seller.

Carriers are those organizations that "transport goods or people, usually over a fixed route and on a fixed schedule" (NIGP Dictionary, 2021); although some airlines offer non-scheduled delivery of goods and passengers based on an hourly rate or per mile/kilometer charge. The primary *modes* include railroads, motor carriers, airlines, water carriers, and pipelines. More on transportation modes can be found in Chapter 3. The supplier or the buying entity may negotiate for transportation and related services depending on the terms of the contract. The party responsible for arranging transportation is the *shipper*.

Beyond basic transportation, shippers may also hire third-party intermediaries which coordinate the various modes of transportation for shipment from supplier to buyer, and may also offer other services. Some examples include transportation brokers, freight forwarders, and shippers' associations. *Transportation brokers* locate carriers for shippers, consolidate shipments, and charge a certain percentage of the rate to the shipper. *Freight forwarders* help with the movement of shipments by combining less-than-carload (LCL) or less-than-truckload (LTL) lots into carload (CL) or truckload (TL) lots. The freight forwarder pays the transportation carrier based on CL or TL rates, but charges the shipper on LCL or LTL rates, which are higher. *Shippers' associations* are not-for-profit organizations that act as freight forwarders. Any profits obtained through the consolidation of shipments are returned to the shippers. There are also *3PLs*, which are firms that provide multiple logistics services for use by customers. Preferably, these services are integrated or bundled together by the provider. *4PLs* go beyond 3PLs, operating under a long-term contract or in a joint venture with the client. The 4PL selects and manages multiple providers. While a 4PL manages a single supply chain, a *5PL* manages a network of supply chains for the client. More on the roles of these providers can be found in Chapter 3.

Transportation is an integral component of logistics, which "is responsible for the movement, routing, distribution, transportation, and coordination activities that apply to goods delivery or service performance" (NIGP, 2021). While *logistics* refers to both the inbound and outbound sides, Procurement is primarily concerned with the inbound movement of goods and services to its internal clients.

Evolution of Logistics

The term *logistics* was derived from military activities related to the deployment and support of armed forces during times of war (Gourdin, 2001). In fact, *logistics* was referenced as early as 500 BC in *The Art of War* (Tzu & Gagliardi, 1999)—a book about logistical activities and their relationship to war tactics and strategies. During World War II, logistical activities contributed to victory for the United States and its allies. Since the 1960s, logistics has gradually moved to the forefront of best business practices. Logistical activities were again identified as a critical component of success for the United States during the Gulf War in 1990–1991, which involved the massive movement of 122 million meals, 1.3 billion gallons of fuel, and 31,800 tons of mail (Pagonis, 1992). Logistical activities have likewise required critical attention in subsequent military engagements.

During the 1960s and 1970s, the impact of global competition on U.S. firms was significant. Companies were losing market share and revenues to firms from other countries, particularly Japan and Germany. Competitive pressures increased in the mid-1970s as trade barriers were reduced, forcing U.S. firms to improve the quality of their products and services, focus on higher levels of customer service and satisfaction, and reduce costs. Logistics spend was identified as the final frontier for cost reduction and improved customer service (Heskett, 1977). More on global transportation can be found in Chapter 6. Businesses turned their attention to the physical distribution of goods and materials to achieve improved customer service and cost savings. They moved toward logistics management—that is, the integration of transportation, distribution, warehousing, finished goods, inventory, management, packaging, and materials handling. Deregulation of transportation played a key role, as increased competition among carriers resulted in lower transportation rates and better management of inbound transportation. More on the deregulation of carriers can be found in Chapter 2.

Beginning in the late 1970s and continuing into the 1980s, physical distribution management evolved into logistics management. This movement led to Purchasing's increased involvement in logistical decisions, including transportation management, and was influenced by changes in the manufacturing environment and an increased emphasis on quality (Gentry, 1991). The environment changed as manufacturers began outsourcing a greater percentage of the content of their products to outside suppliers. These suppliers were able to produce parts at a lower cost—in part because of their non-union environment and related overhead costs, geographic locations, and greater economies of scale due to specializing in a few select items. To replace the benefits of controlling production of all parts, many firms moved to a just-in- time (JIT) manufacturing model. In essence, JIT involved suppliers delivering parts to manufacturing sites when required for production, and producing goods based on actual customer need rather than forecasts, resulting in lower inventory carrying costs. However, it also meant that relationships between suppliers and transportation carriers had to be stronger, to assure delivery within tight windows. In many instances, companies moved to single-sourcing arrangements. At the same time, the total quality management movement was in full force, enabling firms to compete with foreign goods producers. The selection of quality carriers was an important part of the equation, because manufacturers had to be assured that finished goods would be moved safely and customers would be provided a proper level of service. Once firms had reduced the number of carriers in the pool, they focused on developing measures of performance and monitoring carriers more closely. These measures included percentage of on-time shipments, percentage of damaged shipments, and percentage of complete orders shipped.

During the late 1980s and 1990s, the term *supply chain management* was coined to describe the total flow of goods and information from the supplying agency to the final "customer," realizing that each step in the flow of goods should add value (Ellram & Cooper, 1993). The opportunity for savings within a supply chain was the driving factor behind this new trend. A supply chain has a series of "fixed points"—manufacturing sites, warehouses, distribution centers, and offices where goods are stored—linked together by transportation and information exchanges. This strategy included the development of partnerships with manufacturers, suppliers, and logistics-related members of the supply chain, including transportation carriers. In particular, shippers spent more time qualifying their carriers. Carrier strategies that led to more successful relationships within the supply chain (Wagner & Frankel, 2000) included:

- entering into partnerships in which both shipper and carrier challenge each other to provide innovative solutions;
- working jointly with shippers to control transportation costs;

- providing services considered the highest priority by the shipper;
- committing to continuous improvement processes that are critical to positive change;
- implementing satellite communication systems; and
- providing information systems, logistics consulting, and specialized services based on customer needs.

Since 2000, logistics organizations have sought to adapt and refine their performance in a rapidly changing world. Technological advancements such as the Internet, mobile devices, and industry-specific software, along with growth in e-commerce solutions, have made it easier for smaller entities to purchase from global suppliers. However, with globalization and changing political conditions in some countries have come additional risks. Logistics and supply chain managers have added risk analysis to develop alternative solutions in the event of unforeseen events such as natural disasters or global pandemics. Lastly, there is continuing pressure to address the issue of sustainability (Tino, 2020). In essence, logistics companies are seeking to reduce their carbon footprints through measures such as mitigating carbon dioxide (CO_2) emissions, noise pollution, and accidents. More on this topic can be found later in this chapter and in Chapter 8.

Transportation and Logistics Statistics

Logistics costs as a percentage of gross domestic product (GDP) have fallen significantly since the advent of deregulation. From a high of 17.9% in the early 1980s, they had dropped to 7.4% by 2020. Between 2011 and 2020, costs as a percentage were relatively stable, ranging from 7.36% to 7.83% (Gilmore, 2021). Transportation costs are the largest component of logistics costs, and about two-thirds are spent on trucking.

A more complete picture of logistics costs is provided in Figure 1.1, which breaks down where organizations spent their logistics dollars in 2020. Shippers primarily spent most of their dollars (64.7%) on transportation, using trucking as their primary mode. Second in importance were inventory carrying costs, including interest, taxes, insurance, obsolescence, depreciation, and warehousing. A small amount of spend went to shippers' administrative costs and carrier support costs. More on the costs of logistics and transportation can be found in Chapter 4.

Figures also are available on actual expenditures by the Federal, state, and local governments, which support the U.S. transportation infrastructure. As shown in Figure 1.2, the three largest expenditures in 2018 were highway, public transit, and air transportation. Highway expenditure should come as no

Figure 1.1 Logistics costs, 2020

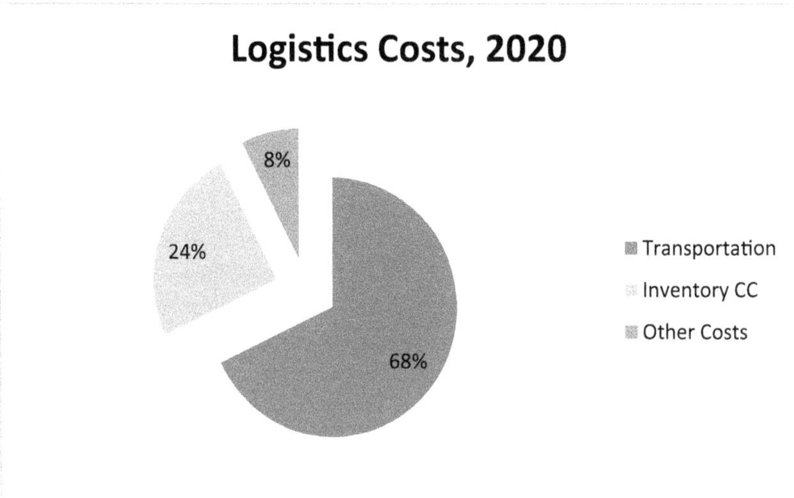

Source: Gilmore, Dan (2021, September). State of the Logistics Union 2021, Supply Chain Digest).

Figure 1.2 Federal, state and local expenditures, 2018

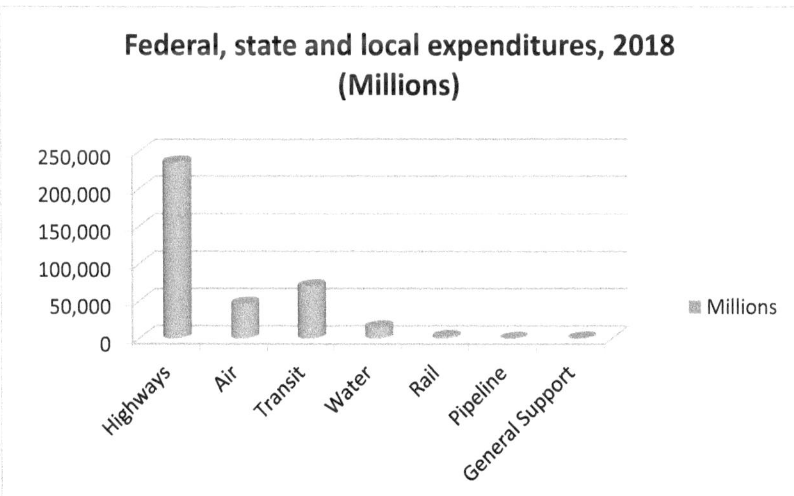

Source: U.S. Department of Transportation, Bureau of Transportation Statistics, www.bts.gov.

surprise, given the amount spent by organizations on trucking shipments. The sums spent on supporting rail, water, and pipelines—as would be expected—were relatively low.

Strategic Planning

The main goal for those managing the logistics function is to provide the best possible service through a combination of customer service, transportation, warehousing, and inventory management activities. It is important that those involved know and understand the entity's overall vision, mission, strategy, goals, and objectives to develop supporting strategies. This can be accomplished through the strategic planning process.

As a management tool, strategic planning is a process by which people make decisions about intended future outcomes, how those outcomes are to be achieved (i.e., strategy), and how success will be measured and evaluated. Strategic planning takes place at the highest level in an entity and should be done on a routine basis. Its purpose is to help the entity reduce costs, improve service, and avoid crisis situations.

Whether an entity has an existing strategic plan or is new to the process, there are certain steps that should be followed, as shown in Figure 1.3. The strategic plan should be created based on the entity's vision and include its mission statement—that is:

- why the entity exists;
- who it serves; and
- the benefits citizens or clients will derive from the services provided.

The vision statement addresses how the entity believes its citizens or clients can best be served. Based on its vision and mission, the entity can more easily develop a set of goals and objectives. Goals address what the entity wants to achieve, while objectives translate those goals into concrete numbers or percentages. The entity should then collect information about the present situation and trends that are expected to impact the entity, whether positive or negative. Next, an analysis of the entity's strengths, weaknesses, opportunities, and threats—known as a SWOT analysis—should be performed. Strengths and weaknesses are those internal factors that affect the viability of the strategic plan, while potential opportunities and threats are external to the entity. Once this information has been analyzed, it will be easier to prioritize any issues raised and create the mission and vision. The entity can then develop its goals and objectives, and have these reviewed by key stakeholders. For example, if the goal is to reduce the entity's carbon footprint, the objective would address the percentage reduction and the timeframe for achieving this. The City of Portland developed a Climate Action Plan in 1993 which aspired to reduce carbon emissions (goal) by 40% by 2030 (objective). In 2018, emissions were down by 19% from 1990 levels (City of Portland, 2021).

Figure 1.3 Strategic planning process

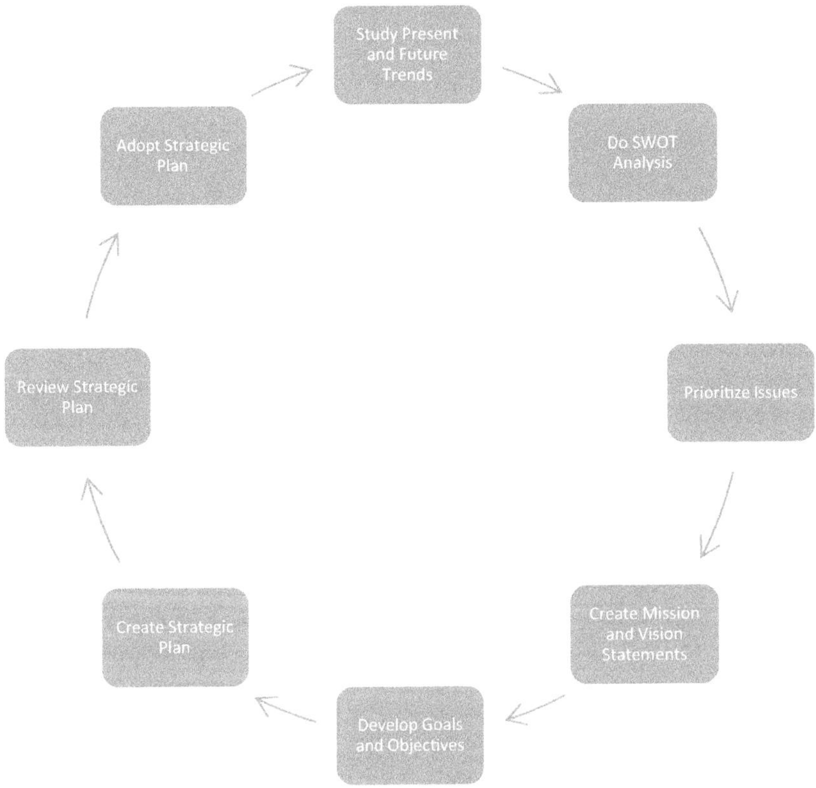

Source: Deeb, G. (2018), "The Top 6 Steps of Strategic Planning," Forbes (December 4). www.forbes.com/sites/georgedeeb/2018/12/04/the-top-6-steps-of-strategic-planning/?sh=3413789035b2.

Once all aspects of the strategic plan have been developed, the plan will be up for review. If everyone is agreeable, the entity will then formally adopt the strategic plan (Deeb, 2018). Depending on the entity and its environment, this process could be done every year or every five years, but the average is every three years.

Logistics Planning

Once the strategic planning process is complete, the logistics planning process follows and should result in a plan that supports the strategic plan. *Logistics planning* has been defined as "a unified, comprehensive, and integrated planning process; anticipating future demand for logistics services such as transportation, facilities, customer service and warehousing; and managing the resources of the entire supply chain (and done within the overall context of the organizational plan)" (Cooper, Innis, & Dickson, 1992). The logistics plan describes how these services will be delivered to the client.

The logistics plan also will cover:

- how the outcomes described in the plan will be achieved;
- what services will be offered;
- how success will be measured and evaluated; and
- how budgetary resources will be allocated.

Several steps are involved in developing a logistics plan (Lambert, Stock, & Ellram, 1998). First, a logistics audit of current performance is necessary. The audit team should include anyone involved in managing or performing logistical activities. This provides the opportunity for the procurement professional to be an active team member. Any gaps in performance should be identified at this time. In many instances, there may be necessary tradeoffs between activities that affect performance.

Similar to strategic planning, those involved in logistics planning should conduct environmental scanning, which involves looking at, and interpreting, information about trends, events, and relationships in an entity's external environment. Some major trends are affecting the way logistics activities are performed and are discussed later in this chapter. For example, blockchain technology is expected to improve data reliability and will be considered a key part of the logistics plan; and artificial intelligence (AI) can potentially uncover problems and offer solutions (Bohdan, 2021). These new forms of technology are discussed further in Chapter 7.

The logistics planning team should also look internally at the various functional areas—such as transportation, inventory management, warehousing, and customer service—and evaluate their performance. From this information, the audit team should be able to develop a list of key issues that need further investigation. For example, the current customer service process may need to be improved; or there may be lost opportunities for cost reduction within the logistics system that need to be addressed. There also may be opportunities to outsource some or all logistics activities. Once this list has been developed, it is important to determine if logistics is meeting the entity's goals and objectives. To assess current performance, some concrete measures will be needed. These measures should cover the effectiveness of customer service, such as order cycle times and delivery performance; the cost efficiency of logistics—that is, looking at the costs of inventory management, warehousing, purchasing, and transportation; and an assessment of how well assets are being utilized, including inventory, warehouses and other storage facilities, and any transportation equipment.

Surveying or interviewing internal and external stakeholders is also important to determine if the current logistics system is meeting end user needs and if requirements may be changing in the future. Documentation should include inputs on current performance, including bills of lading, freight bills, order cycle times data, and fill rate data. This information can then be compiled into a standardized format, possibly in a database or spreadsheets.

Once all surveys, interviews, and data have been collected, they should be analyzed in light of the original issues raised. A proposed strategy and its expected impact on service levels can then be developed. Examples of strategies include cost reduction, reduced capital investment, and service improvement. These strategic and logistical planning activities are important processes that can lead to better organizational and logistical performance. The following case study gives a glimpse of the process at New Jersey's Department of Transportation.

Case Study: Freight Planning in the State of New Jersey

In 2007 the New Jersey Department of Transportation (NJDOT) created its first comprehensive plan for freight, which provided a picture of its freight transportation network, operational and policy issues, and general needs. The plan was updated in 2017 and was a blueprint for NJDOT's investment in freight infrastructure. The plan identifies New Jersey's mission, which states that NJDOT will provide a world-class transportation system that:

- enhances the quality of life for residents and the traveling public;
- achieves consistent progress through focused investment in keeping infrastructure in a state of good repair;
- stimulates and sustains smart development and economic growth;
- employs the latest technologies to adapt to changing conditions and environments;
- respects and protects the distinctive and delicate character of the state's natural resources; and
- eagerly embraces its role as a customer service organization.

From the mission statement, NJDOT established its goals, including the following:

- Improve safety and security;
- Improve reliability and efficiency;
- Maintain and renew infrastructure;
- Leverage innovative technologies and practices; and
- Support environmental stewardship, local communities and quality of life.

Objectives were then created to support these goals. A strategic freight plan was then developed, which consisted of applying for freight-specific federal funding opportunities and laying out a series of projects to support the mission, goals, and objectives.

Source: State of New Jersey (2017). 2017 Statewide Freight Plan. www.state.nj.us/transportation/freight/plan/stateplan17.shtm.

Trends in Logistics and Transportation

Logistics and transportation have played an important role in the development of the United States and thus its economy. City locations and their growth were often influenced by access to transportation. For example, Boston initially grew because of its origins as a port city; Chicago was a hub for the railroads; Atlanta—initially a railroad stop—now has the world's largest airport for passenger service; while Memphis has the largest airport for cargo transit. Today, significant changes are occurring within the industry itself. Players in this formerly heavily regulated industry now have the freedom to set prices, determine where they want to operate or discontinue service, and negotiate special services for customers. There are also more recent trends to consider.

The 2020/2021 global Covid-19 pandemic significantly changed the way organizations view logistics and supply chains, resulting in greater adoption of new technologies and processes to handle the demands of consumers, nonprofits, and government entities. Investment in blockchain technology has skyrocketed since 2019 and is expected to increase more than fourfold by 2022. Blockchain uses a public ledger system that records all changes to a record. For example, each movement of a container can be recorded, allowing shippers to reroute for greater efficiency and minimize delivery steps (Daley, 2021).

Beyond blockchain, organizations are investing in other technologies, including digital training solutions, Internet of Things (IoT), and cloud computing. Digital training solutions help with worker recruitment, hiring and training when the need is high, and appeal to a younger workforce. IoT has driven improvements in warehouses. In essence, it connects all devices so that data can be shared and monitored using the Internet. For warehouses, devices include robots, drones, pallets, and inventory (Anonymous, 2021b). Cloud computing minimizes communication problems, strengthens collaboration in a safe way, and helps logistics providers improve their processes because data collection and analysis is easier. More on advances in technology can be found in Chapter 7.

Reverse logistics activities have also increased. This market was valued at $635.6 billion in 2020 and is expected to grow to $958.3 billion by 2028, despite a dip in 2021 (Halmar et al., 2021). Reverse logistics activities include returns, refurbishment, repairs, recycling and disposal. Some organizations also use this as an opportunity to benefit others. Campbell Soup Company, for example, partners with food banks and a third-party logistics provider to distribute its products to those in need (see case study below).

Case Study: Partnering in Tough Times

Founded in 1869, Campbell Soup Company is "a focus-brand powerhouse with two divisions, Meals & Snacks, and Beverages." In March 2020, the company made a commitment to donate food and money to 33 food banks across the United States in response to the pandemic. At the time, many food banks were stretched to provide enough food to those in need. They were also shifting from direct delivery to other options, such as mobile pantries and meal delivery, to meet the needs of their clients. Two of these non-profits—Feeding Tampa Bay and Utah Food Bank—were not easy to reach from one of Campbell's distribution centers. In response, one of its carrier partners and a 3PL, NFI, generously donated its services to deliver the food.

Source: Campbell's Soup Company (2021). A Neighborly Partnership to Support Our Communities (April 13). www.campbellsoupcompany.com/newsroom/news/a-neighborly-partnership-to-support-our-communities/.

Lastly, sustainable logistical and supply practices aimed at reducing ecological footprints have become increasingly important, mainly driven by consumers.

Better collaboration between government and business partners, integration of logistics and supply chain processes, use of alternative fuels, and eco-driving education are just some of the ways that improvements can be made. Local governments are also implementing strategies to help the environment. See Chapter 8 for more on environmental issues.

The year 2021 also brought challenges that are expected to extend out for at least two years. For example, U.S. companies experienced shortages of factory workers, truck drivers, dock workers, and warehouse workers due to concerns about the spread of Covid-19 and an aging workforce (Connerly, 2021). The result has been disruptions in logistics hubs and delivery problems. Globally, factories in several Southeast Asian countries were in lockdown due to a significant increase in Covid-19 cases, negatively impacting supply chains (Deutsche Welle, 2021).

Conclusions

Over 50 years ago, logistics was identified as an area of significance in the procurement cycle. Since then, much has been learned and the field of logistics is an exciting one today, even with its challenges. This chapter introduced the subject of logistics and transportation, with definitions of several transportation terms, a short history of the evolution of logistics into its present form, some important statistics, a description of the strategic planning process, and an outline of current trends. Demand for transportation in the aviation, rail, and trucking sectors is expected to grow, while new opportunities will continue for 3PLs that offer various services related to transportation. However, global pandemics, worker shortages, climate change, and natural disasters will remain a challenge. Multiple opportunities are available to improve logistics performance, particularly with technological advancements. Whether directly or indirectly involved in logistics activities, the reader will hopefully gain an appreciation of the field and realize its importance to Procurement in the following chapters. Greater involvement in transportation and logistics decisions can lead to improved service and increased savings for Procurement's "customers," whether internal or external.

References

Anonymous (2016a). "3PLs and Carriers: At Your Service," Inbound Logistics, December 29. www.inboundlogistics.com/cms/article/3pls-carriers-at-your-service/.

Anonymous (2021b). "5 Warehouse Automation Trends 2021 and Beyond", The European Business Review, May 8. www.europeanbusinessreview.com/5-warehouse-automation-trends-for-2021-and-beyond/.

Bohdan, A. (2021). "Top 6 Global Logistics Technology Trends in 2021," Supply and Demand Chain Executive, March 31. www.sdcexec.com/transportation/article/21307643/amconsoft-top-6-global-logistic-technology-trends-in-2021.

City of Portland. "History and key documents of climate planning and action in Portland." www.portland.gov/bps/climate-action/history-and-key-documents.

Connerly, B. (2021). "The Labor Shortage is Why Supply Chains are Disrupted", Forbes, July 7. www.forbes.com/sites/billconerly/2021/07/07/the-labor-shortage-is-why-supply-chains-are-disrupted/?sh=714d1952301d.

Cooper, M. C., Innis, D. E., & Dickson, P. R. (1992). *Strategic Planning for Logistics*. Oak Brook, IL: Council of Logistics Management.

Daley, S. (2021). "Making Moves: 21 Companies Using Blockchain's Logistics Capabilities to Excel," Builtin Beta, May 6. https://builtin.com/blockchain/blockchain-supply-chain-logistics-uses.

Deeb, G. (2018). "The Top 6 Steps of Strategic Planning, Forbes, December 4. www.forbes.com/sites/georgedeeb/2018/12/04/the-top-6-steps-of-strategic-planning/?sh=3413789035b2.

Deutsche Welle (DW) (2021). "COVID Surge in Southeast Asia Disrupts Global Supply Chains," September 5. www.dw.com/en/covid-surge-in-southeast-asia-disrupts-global-supply-chains/a-59062324.

Ellram, L. M., & Cooper, M. C. (1993). "Characteristics of supply chain management and the implications for purchasing and logistics strategy." International Journal of Logistics Management, 4(2), 13–24.

Gentry, J. J. (1991). *Purchasing's Involvement in Transportation Decision Making*. Tempe, AZ: Center for Advanced Purchasing Studies.

Gilmore, D. (2021). "State of the Logistics Union 2021," Supply Chain Digest, June 25. www.scdigest.com/firstthoughts/21-06-25_State_of_Logistics_Report_Review_Comment.php?cid=18798.

Gourdin, K. N. (2001). *Global Logistics Management*. Oxford, UK: Blackwell Publishers, Ltd.

Halmare, M., Chandra, A. and Mutreja, S. (2021). "Reverse Logistics Market," Allied Market Research, July. www.alliedmarketresearch.com/reverse-logistics-market.

Heskett, J. L. (1977). "Logistics—Essential to strategy," *Harvard Business Review*, November/December, 84–95.

Johnson, P.F. (2020). *Purchasing and Supply Management*. New York: McGraw-Hill Education.

Lambert, D. M., Stock, J. R., & Ellram, L. M. (1998). *Fundamentals of Logistics Management*. Boston: Irwin McGraw-Hill.

NIGP (2021). Dictionary of Terms. www.nigp.org/dictionary-of-terms.

Pagonis, W. G. (1992). *Moving Mountains: Lessons in Leadership and Logistics from the Gulf War*. Boston, MA: Harvard Business School Publishing.

Tino, G. (2020). "Supply Chain and Logistics: 20 Years of Change," February 13, Jobsinlogistics.com.

Tzu, S., & Gagliardi, G. (1999). *The Art of War: In Sun Tzu's Own Words*. Seattle, WA: Clearbridge Publishing.

Wagner, W. B., & Frankel, R. (2000). "Quality carriers: Critical link in supply chain relationship development." International Journal of Logistics: Research and Applications, 3(3), 245–257.

Wood, D. F., & Johnson, J. C. (1995) *Contemporary Transportation* (5th ed.). Upper Saddle River, NJ: Prentice Hall.

Chapter 2

Transportation Law

Introduction

The U.S. government has played a significant role in the transportation policies that provide infrastructure such as roads, bridges, canals, ports, airports, and rights of way. It also manages traffic through road safety regulations and rules enforced by the Federal Aviation Administration (FAA) to ensure the smooth flow of air traffic. Another important influence on how carriers transport goods has been the degree of regulation. There are four ways in which the U.S. government regulates carriers:

- economic regulation, which relates to the rates carriers can charge;
- service regulation, which ensures that carriers provide services consistent with their operating rights;
- safety regulation, such as drug testing, which falls under the Department of Transportation (DOT) and the Occupational Safety and Health Administration; and
- environmental regulation, which affects activities such as disposal of municipal and industrial waste.

Why this degree of regulation? The government wants to encourage and advance the economic development of transportation—that is, to promote transportation to the public. For example, the mission of DOT is "to ensure America has the safest, most efficient and modern transportation system in the world, which boosts our economic productivity and global competitiveness

DOI: 10.4324/9781003298625-2

and enhances the quality of life in communities both rural and urban" (transportation.gov). Its priorities are safety, innovation, and infrastructure; to this end, in 2021, several programs were established with aims such as preventing human trafficking, advancing technology transfer, and offering grants to improve U.S. infrastructure. Another goal of the federal government is to ensure that all transportation carriers operate fairly and do not discriminate. Transportation laws still include the "common carrier obligation," which requires common carriers (i.e., those classified as providing service to all within a certain area) to provide the following:

- Service: Serve all customers that request their service;
- Delivery: Deliver goods, with reasonable dispatch, in the same condition as when the carrier picked them up;
- Reasonable rates; and
- Fair treatment: Avoid discrimination and treat all customers, products, and geographic locations the same.

Because some of these regulations are still being utilized, it is important to have a good understanding of the legislation proposed and enacted over the past 140 years.

History of Transportation Regulation

Railroads

Regulation of the transportation industry was initiated in response to abuses of economic power in the railroad industry that began in the 1860s. While railroads had been operating along the East Coast since the 1830s, the lure of the West was great for both entrepreneurs and the U.S. Government. Industrialists wanted to increase their wealth through access to the West's natural resources, such as gold, silver, and lumber. The Federal Government wanted control of California during the Civil War to gain an advantage over the Confederacy. Railroad transportation was the most efficient and available means to link the East with the West.

With that in mind, the U.S. Government enacted major legislation from the 1860s to the 1970s to promote and control the railroad industry (see Figure 2.1). The first piece of legislation was the Pacific Railway Act, passed in 1862, which provided government bonds and granted public land—known as land grants—to the Union Pacific and Central Pacific Railroads for every mile of track laid from Nebraska to California. Other railroads, realizing an opportunity for

Figure 2.1 Major railroad legislation, 1882–1976

Year	*Act*	*Purpose*
1882	Pacific Railway Act	Expansion of railroads
1887	Act to Regulate Commerce	Prevent intrastate regulation; create ICC
1903	Elkins Anti-Rebating Act	Broaden ICC's powers
1906	Hepburn Act	Further broaden ICC's powers
1910	Mann-Elkins Act	Give ICC authority to suspend rates for up to ten months
1920	Transportation Act	Give ICC authority to prescribe minimum rates
1933	Emergency Railroad Transportation Act	Created position of Transportation Coordinator
1973	Regional Rail Reorganization Act (3-R Act)	Restructure bankrupt railroads
1976	Railroad Revitalization Regulatory Reform Act (4-R Act)	Restore the railroad industry

federal funding, soon started competing with the two railroads for these land grants. From 1862 to 1871, more than 100 million acres of land were granted to private railroad companies and the transcontinental railroad was successfully completed. Railroads became the most important service from the late 1800s to the early 1900s, surpassing the use of waterways (U.S. Senate, 2021).

Regulation of the railroads did not begin until 1877, following extensive abuse of the railroads' monopoly after the Civil War. Small towns, in particular, suffered from high rates. The railroads also offered better rates to their favorite customers, which included the monopolists in the coal, steel, and iron markets. Rebates of 50% to 80% of the published rate to favored shippers were not uncommon, forcing out competitors which were paying higher rates. Another common practice among the railroads was bribery of those in power—such as judges, senators, and governors—to assure that these common abuses of power continued. Lastly, the railroads manipulated their stock and bond prices: to finance the construction of railroad tracks and equipment, they sold stock at inflated prices to unwary investors. This scheme involved "construction companies" that were created and owned by the railroads, which overestimated the costs of construction. These estimates were used to justify stock prices to investors. Investments were sold to unwary investors at rates equal to the inflated costs of construction. Investor funds were then deposited with the construction company, which subcontracted the work to others at actual cost, with any differences pocketed by the railroad.

Several Midwestern states responded by passing "Granger laws," which regulated transportation within their states. These laws were contested in several cases that reached the U.S. Supreme Court. In *Munn v. Illinois* (1877), the Supreme Court ruled that state governments could regulate rates "affected with the public interest" —that is, states could regulate interstate railroad rates. *Interstate rates* refer to rates charged for freight moved between states, while *intrastate rates* are rates charged for freight movements within one state.

However, in *Wabash v. Illinois* (1886) (formerly known as *Wabash, St. Louis and Pacific Railroad Company v. Illinois*), the Supreme Court determined that states could not regulate the intrastate portion of interstate shipments; federal action was required. As a result, Congress passed the Act to Regulate Commerce (1887). Key elements of the law included the following:

- All interstate or foreign railroad service fell under federal regulation.
- The Interstate Commerce Commission (ICC) was created to administer the law. Its activities included:
  - interpreting the law;
  - setting rates; and
  - issuing mandates.
- Common carrier obligations now fell under the jurisdiction of the ICC.
- Rates had to be "reasonable and just."
- Rate discrimination was outlawed.
- Joint ratemaking among railroads was legal.

Through this Act, carriers were allowed to jointly establish prices for a specific region or geographic area through "rate bureaus," which were organizations maintained by common carriers. The railroads actually supported regulation because competition was increasing, and they wanted to prevent their rates from dropping further.

Major transportation legislation was enacted again in the early 1900s, with the initial passage of the Elkins Anti-Rebating Act (1903), which broadened the base of power of the ICC. This Act made rates published by the ICC the "official" rates. The Hepburn Act (1906) gave the ICC broader powers to review rate complaints and replace an existing rate with one deemed reasonable and just; however, the ICC remained aligned with the basic rate structure already in place. This Act also regulated oil pipelines, an emerging mode of transportation, under the Act to Regulate Commerce.

The Mann-Elkins Act (1910) gave the ICC new powers to suspend rate increases for up to 10 months while it ran any type of investigation. This Act was the result of the railroad industry's attempt to raise rates to improve profitability. However, realizing that railroads were in financial straits following World War I, Congress passed the Transportation Act of 1920, allowing the ICC to prescribe minimum rates.

The Great Depression of the 1930s led to even more financial problems for the railroads, due to reduced demand and increased competition from motor carriers. In 1933, the Emergency Railroad Transportation Act was passed, which created a Federal Transportation Coordinator to oversee the industry. The Transportation Coordinator did not do much to improve the industry, but his reports to Congress led to the Motor Carrier Act of 1935, which regulated the trucking and bus industries.

No further railroad regulation occurred until the 1970s. At that time, the railroads were in serious financial trouble, and only two major carriers were profitable. Several railroads in the Northeast filed for receivership, which was blamed on too much regulation. Congress initially passed the Regional Rail Reorganization Act in 1973, creating the United States Railway Association, which was charged with restructuring the bankrupt railroads. The Consolidated Rail Corporation (Conrail), a semi-public company, was also formed to manage the restructured railroad system. A second act, the Railroad Revitalization and Regulatory Reform Act ("4-R Act"), was passed in 1976. Its priorities were to restore the railroads' financial stability, upgrade and maintain the railway infrastructure, and promote the railroads to the public.

Circumstances also led to the regulation of other modes of transportation, as shown in Figure 2.2 and discussed in the following sections.

Motor Carriage

The invention of the automobile led to a new form of competition and threat to the railroads: motor carriage. Between 1914 and 1931, the railroad industry filed multiple lawsuits against trucking firms and applied pressure to state legislatures, resulting in state regulation of trucks and buses. However, the Supreme Court ruled in the 1920s that states could not regulate interstate transportation. In an attempt to restrict competition and avoid federal regulation, motor carriers banded together and developed their own rules of good conduct, which was legal at the time under the National Industrial Recovery Act of 1933. Nevertheless, the Supreme Court ruled the Act unconstitutional in 1935. Up to this point, the trucking industry had opposed regulation; but to

Figure 2.2 Major regulatory acts—motor carriage, air, and water

Mode	*Year*	*Act*	*Purpose*
Motor carriage	1935	Motor Carrier Act	ICC to regulate motor carriers
	1958	Transportation Act	Extend regulation to frozen foods
Air	1926	Air Commerce Act	Secretary of Commerce assigned to set and enforce rules, certifications and airways
	1940	Transportation Act	CAA and CAB to regulate air transport
	1958	Transportation Act	Regulatory authority transferred to FAA
Water	1904	Cargo Preference Act	Provide business to U.S. flag ships
	1916	Shipping Act	Stabilize the industry
	1920	Merchant Marine Act	Domestic transport must be done by U.S.-owned carriers on U.S.-built vessels
	1940	Transportation Act	Carriers placed under ICC to regulate rates and service

protect itself, it changed its position, and Congress passed the Motor Carrier Act of 1935.

Under this Act, the motor carrier industry and brokers were placed within the oversight of the ICC. Five types of service were recognized: common, contract, private, exempt, and brokerage. As in the railroad industry, common carriers served the general public and charged according to published rates, known as *tariffs*. Contract carriers could negotiate a contract rate with shippers on an individual basis. Private carriers owned the goods they moved and were not for hire to others. Exempt carriers—for-hire transportation companies moving goods that were not subject to economic regulation—were still required to meet safety standards. Brokers acted as third parties by arranging for and selling transportation services for carriers. To control market entry, common carriers were required to possess a *certificate of operating rights*, stating the authorized routes they could serve. New carriers were also required to carry a *certificate of public convenience*, and limitations could be placed on a carrier based on its documentation of previous service. All rates had to be filed with the ICC 30 days prior to their effective date, and tariffs were published and made available to all. Proposed tariffs had to cover the full costs of transportation, according to ICC estimates, or were rejected. An exemption was allowed for trucks carrying agricultural products.

If a common carrier was in operation as of June 1, 1935, it was *grandfathered* in—that is, allowed to continue to serve existing routes. However, its expansion of authority was limited. Only if a route was not already served would the ICC consider extending a license. The purpose of this clause was to prevent new competitors from entering a route already served by existing carrier(s). The end result was the buying and selling of rights to routes to and from existing carriers. It also created inefficiencies. If Carrier A had the authority to move freight from City A to City B and purchased rights to move freight from City B to City C, Carrier A was required to carry goods originating from City A and bound for City C through City B, even if a shorter route existed between City A and City C.

The Transportation Act of 1958 extended motor carrier regulation to include frozen foods. This Act also contained a national transportation policy directing the ICC to be fair and impartial in its regulation of all modes and preserve the inherent advantages of each (mode). In other words, the ICC should not allow any mode to be driven out of a market.

Air Transportation

Air travel was also on the upswing with the invention of aircraft large enough to move people and freight. With the passage of the Air Commerce Act of 1926—a central piece of legislation for airline regulation—the Department of Commerce was given authority to regulate air commerce, air traffic, and air safety.

From 1927 to 1938, the airline industry experienced substantial growth. By 1938 there were 17 major carriers, but they were concerned about competition from the railroads, the dominant mode of transportation at the time. As a result, they sought federal aid and protection from "excessive competition." The Air Transport Association (ATA), a trade group, was created in 1936 and helped develop the Civil Aeronautics Act of 1938 to regulate fares, routes, and new entry. Regulation of airways transferred from the Department of Commerce to the Civil Aeronautics Authority (CAA).

The Transportation Act of 1940 included changes to the airline industry. Regulatory authority over airlines was split between the CAA, which regulated air traffic and air safety enforcement; and the Civil Aeronautics Board (CAB), which was given the authority to set safety rules, investigate accidents, and regulate economics. Later, the Transportation Act of 1958 transferred the duties of the CAA to a newly created agency, the Federal Aviation Agency (FAA). The FAA exists to this day.

Water

Since early civilization, transporting goods by water carriage—whether across seas, rivers, or lakes, through canals or some combination—has been an important mode of transportation because it allows bulky items and containers to be moved at a low cost compared to other modes. Ancient Egyptians used natural waterways and manmade canals, and built ports to receive and dispatch goods. More recently, the United States experienced the "golden age" of shipping from 1830 to 1860; but thereafter, cargo shipments ebbed until 1914 due to poor policies and legislation. The Shipping Act of 1916 created the U.S. Shipping Board, whose mission was to stabilize the ocean carrier industry and reinvigorate the Merchant Marine.

As a result of World War I, there were concerns about national defense and economic security, resulting in the Merchant Marine Act of 1920 (also known as the Jones Act). This act contained a requirement that carriers transporting cargo point to point within the United States, even via foreign ports, be owned by U.S. citizens, and required the vessels to be registered in the United States. Another requirement was that vessels be built in the United States. These requirements could be waived, but only in unusual circumstances (U.S. Department of Transportation Maritime Division, 2021).

No other major legislation affecting water transportation was passed until the Transportation Act of 1940, which placed domestic water carriers under ICC rate and service regulation. Exemptions were allowed for carriers moving three or fewer dry-bulk commodities on one barge or several barges tied together, and for movements of liquid bulk products (which covered about 90% of all domestic water shipments).

The United States also enacted cargo preference laws to protect and promote U.S. flag carriers. For example, the Military Cargo Preference Act of 1904 required U.S. contractors to use U.S. flag carriers 100% of the time when the cargo was procured for the military or the Export Import Bank. The Cargo Preference Act of 1954 required cargo procured for civilian entities or agricultural needs to be shipped using U.S. flag carriers at least 50% of the time (U.S. Department of Transportation Maritime Division, 2021).

The Federal Maritime Commission (FMC) was created in 1961 to regulate overseas shipping of U.S. ocean carriers and investigate their practices and those of freight operators. It also reviews tariff publications under the Shipping Act of 1916.

Beyond U.S. regulation, the International Maritime Organization (IMO), a United Nations (UN) agency, regulates international shipments of its member nations by creating a regulatory framework for the shipping industry. It oversees activities such as ship design and construction, manning, operations, and disposal (International Maritime Organization, 2021).

Other Major Regulatory Legislation

Freight forwarders consolidate small shipments from several shippers into TL or CL lots, and deliver them to carriers for shipment. The Freight Forwarder Act of 1942 added freight forwarders to the list of those covered under federal regulation, stating that they were subject to the Interstate Commerce Act. In effect, entry control, rate and service requirements were regulated. Freight forwarders could not own or control any railroad, oil pipeline, motor carrier or water carrier; but they could own or control other freight forwarders.

The Reed-Bullwinkle Act of 1948 created a new layer of regulation for common carriers by authorizing the use of rate bureaus for all land common carriers. Rate bureaus set rates, but carriers also had the right to establish their own rates if they did not want to participate. Rate bureaus were exempt from antitrust laws.

Impact of Regulation

By the 1970s, the evidence was mounting against continued regulation of motor and air transportation. First, there were significant costs attached to regulation in terms of empty backhauls for motor carriers because routes and products were narrowly specified. Truckers authorized to carry products one way might not be authorized to carry any products on their return trip—the backhaul—resulting in costs attached to moving an empty truck and no offsetting revenue. Second, there often were significant differences in trucking rates between movements of exempt products and near-equivalent regulated products. For example, the variation in tariffs between uncooked and cooked poultry was 50% (Moore, 1995). As a result, the share of total traffic carried by exempt carriers increased not only because of lower rates, but because exempt carriers were better able to meet shippers' needs.

Movement of air cargo also was complicated because the CAB controlled each airline's route structure. Interline agreements between two or more passenger airlines often were needed to deliver cargo along with separately owned motor carriers, which were also heavily regulated. (Under regulatory law, an entity could not own both an airline and a trucking company.) As a result, cargo forwarders were used to coordinate these shipments and also were regulated. All-cargo carriers like FedEx Corporation (FedEx) also were heavily restricted because they fell under the same regulatory structure. Finally, union workers in both the motor carrier and airline industries negotiated large pay increases on a regular basis, which added to the cost of transportation.

Several other factors forced Congress to repeal much of the regulation over these two industries. Ralph Nader, a young activist at the time, and his "Nader's Raiders" were visibly critical of regulatory agencies. A national fuel crisis also resulted in scrutiny of the transportation industry's excessive fuel consumption and led Congress to the conclusion that regulatory policies were at fault. University economists had been strongly opposed to regulation of the trucking industry as early as 1928, and their opposition continued into the late 1970s. They argued that under competitive pricing, rates would be driven down, whereas regulation meant carriers would always force rates up to meet costs. With regulation, they argued, there was no reason to contain costs.

DOT, Congress, and the Department of Justice were strongly in favor of truck deregulation and, as a result, the National Transportation Policy Study Commission (an independent commission) was formed. Its findings resulted in a recommendation that regulatory reform be made a priority item. Although the ICC initially took the position that regulation was needed to ensure a stable industry, it began a series of reforms on its own after Congressional and public debates.

The trucking industry as a whole and the Teamsters in particular were against deregulation. The Teamsters realized that deregulation would lessen their power and result in fewer union jobs. However, different transportation interest groups favored certain reforms. Large shippers were generally in favor of deregulation, but smaller shippers and rural areas were against it because of worries over loss of service.

With several railroads in the Northeast in bankruptcy, changes to the laws regarding the railroads were prompted by concerns over the future viability of the industry. Congress realized that changes were occurring in the marketplace:

- Most transportation in the United States was already very competitive;
- Government regulation, for the most part, had become unnecessary and inefficient;
- Most intercity freight was transported by modes other than rail; and
- Railroad earnings were the lowest of all modes and insufficient to make the capital improvements needed to survive.

(Sampson, Farris, & Shrock, 1981)

As a result, it was determined that new legislation was needed.

The push for economic deregulation of the airlines came with the appointment of economist Alfred E. Kahn as chairman of the CAB. His mission was to eliminate all regulation. At that time, airfares were high, which limited access and choices for the general public.

Deregulation of the Transportation Industry

Air Transportation

While much of the national debate centered on the trucking industry, the first mode to be deregulated was the airline industry, which at the time consisted of 10 major carriers and other regional carriers. In 1976, the CAB started loosening restrictions on the airlines, which was accelerated under Alfred E. Kahn as CAB chairman. Air cargo rates were deregulated with the signing of the Air Transportation Regulatory Reform Act of 1977. The following year President Carter signed the Airline Deregulation Act of 1978, which instructed the CAB to focus on regulatory decisions that advocated competition while preserving service to small communities. Airlines were now automatically allowed to enter markets served by the competition. This opened up the air cargo market, allowing airlines to expand their route structure and to transport cargo without the need for interlining or cargo forwarders. It also freed up all-cargo carriers like FedEx and United Parcel Service (UPS) to buy larger aircraft and develop new markets.

Passenger fares were no longer regulated, and airlines were not required to file rate changes. Discount fares were allowed for the first time. The legislation also included a "sunset clause" for the CAB, requiring it to disband by January 1, 1985. In 1978, the ICC also enlarged airport zones to give airline trucks expanded areas for pickup and delivery.

Motor Carrier Act of 1980

The trucking industry was deregulated, but not as extensively as the airline industry. Market entry was opened to any carrier that could:

- prove its financial ability to take on an operation—that is, that could prove itself fit, willing, and able; and
- verify that the proposed service would serve a useful purpose.

A Master Certificate System was created in which any carrier deemed fit, willing, and able would automatically be granted a certificate for any community not regularly served by a common carrier. Certificates applied to U.S. government freight, vehicles for small packages (i.e., less than 100 pounds), and owner-operated vehicles for food and edible products if the tonnage did not exceed that of exempt products. To protect shippers, all carriers were now required to carry at least $75,000 of insurance—a figure which was increased if the carrier moved hazardous materials.

Controls on rates were loosened with the creation of a "zone of rate freedom." Carriers were now allowed to increase/decrease rates by 10% each year without the approval of the ICC and by an additional 5% at the discretion of the ICC. After two years, changes in rates would be tied to the producers' price index (PPI). Carriers could discuss and vote on general rate increases but not on single-line rate proposals.

The distinctions among classes of carriers also blurred. Contract carriers, previously limited to a maximum of eight customers, were no longer subject to limits. Additionally, private carriers could now carry freight for wholly owned subsidiaries of the same corporation. Further, to alleviate the backhaul problem, the number of products classified as "exempt" was expanded. This clause improved backhaul opportunities for those carriers primarily moving agricultural products to market.

As a result, there was a significant increase in the number of small interstate motor carriers. Approximately half of all TL carriers filed for bankruptcy between 1980 and 1989; but since then, the market has grown. In 2017, there were over 500,000 trucking companies, 80% of which were classified as small businesses (Mall, 2019). Rates declined by approximately 25% from 1977 to 1983 and contributed to the number of bankrupt carriers. Service levels have since increased; but, as predicted by the unions, there has been a significant increase in non-union workers. Deregulation also opened up intermodal service, allowing train cars to carry truck trailers.

Congress completed deregulation of the trucking industry through the Federal Aviation Administration Authorization Act of 1994, which eliminated state regulation of intrastate trucking rates, and the ICC Termination Act of 1995. Transportation regulation was placed with the Surface Transportation Board (STB) under DOT. The ICC Termination Act and the Trucking Industry Regulatory Reform Act (TIRRA) resulted in the elimination of the distinction between common and contract carriers. Tariff filing and rate regulations were repealed, with the exception of movement of household goods or those affecting noncontiguous domestic trade. The STB has broad exemption authority over cargo loss and damage, insurance, safety, fitness, and antitrust immunity; while registration of motor carriers now falls under DOT. Certificates of operating authority are no longer required. A carrier must prove safety, fitness, and financial responsibility only. However, some groups are still excluded from deregulation, including buses, household goods movers, and garbage haulers.

In 1994, the TIRRA also was passed, eliminating the filing requirements for common carriers using individually determined rates versus bureau-set rates. Individually determined rates are those set by a carrier for service provided on its own line. Carriers must keep a list of these individual tariffs and provide them to any existing or potential shipper upon request.

Maislin v. Primary Steel

Because of changes in control over rates and a surge in competition, motor carriers often negotiated rates far below the published tariffs to gain business, but never filed these rates with the ICC. Millions of dollars in undercharges (the difference between the negotiated and published rates) were discovered during financial audits of multiple trucking firms. As a result, carriers in bankruptcy attempted to collect these undercharges, and eventually the legality of this practice was tested before the Supreme Court in 1990. In *Maislin v. Primary Steel* (1989), the court upheld the "filed rate doctrine" of the Elkins Act of 1903, which stated that common carrier negotiated rates were legal only if published in a tariff by the ICC.

The Negotiated Rates Act of 1993 (NRA) was an outcome of the Supreme Court's decision. Under the Act, shippers would now have the option of settling undercharges by paying 15% of the claim amount on TL shipments (greater than 10,000 pounds) or 20% on LTL shipments to the party that claimed it was damaged by the undercharges.

Railroads

The 4-R Act was passed in 1976. The purpose of the Act was twofold: to rescue the railroad industry in the Northeast and to reform past regulation. Changing demographics in the Northeast had resulted in excess rail capacity and a greater need for short-haul movements. The railroads' cost structure was high because of expensive labor contracts and track repair. As a result, freight rates were high. Several railroads had already filed for bankruptcy. The first part of the Act created the United States Railway Association with responsibility for planning and financing the restructuring of these bankrupt railroads. Conrail was created to operate the restructured railroad system.

Regulatory reforms included the establishment of a zone of rate freedom, which allowed railroads to raise or lower rates without prior ICC approval by 7% from beginning-of-the- year rates if they did not "dominate" the market. A railroad was considered to dominate the market if one of the following conditions existed:

- The carrier controlled at least 70% of the traffic;
- The proposed rate was at least 160% or more of the carrier's variable costs; or
- Shippers were locked into shipping with the carrier because of substantial investment in the carrier's facilities.

Rates equal to or greater than variable costs could not be considered "too low" and thus were reasonable. However, no rate could be considered "too high" by the ICC unless it was determined that the railroad dominated that particular market. The ICC was required to shorten the length of time taken to make decisions on proposals, such as rates changes or mergers. The Staggers Rail Act of 1980 followed, continuing a focus on improving the financial viability of the railroads. It was a long and complicated 78-page document with 61 sections. The definition of "market dominance" was specified as 160% of variable costs in 1981, increasing by 5% per year until 1984 to a maximum of 180%. A centerpiece of the Act was the creation of a "zone of rate flexibility" to increase a carrier's freedom in setting rates. If rates were greater than a carrier's variable costs, it could adjust its rates equal to inflation plus 6%, with a maximum of 18% until 1984. After January 1984, carriers could increase rates by inflation plus 4% per year if the railroad had market dominance. Maximum rates were no longer subject to ICC controls if the railroad did not have "market dominance"—that is, situations where the railroad controlled the market or where rates exceeded 160% of variable costs. Rates could then be set freely. However, if the railroad did have market dominance, the ICC could regulate rates when they appeared to exceed 160% of variable costs. Contract rates were legalized. Railroads could now contract with shippers for up to 40% of their capacity, although contracts had to be filed and approved by the ICC. Shippers could protest rates but were limited to allegations that rates would impair the railroad's ability to serve other shippers. Competing carriers could not oppose contracts. Under the ICC Termination Act of 1995, railroad mergers are now reviewed by the STB. Tariff filings and most contract filings for carriers have been eliminated. However, any rate increases or changes in service must be filed with 20 days' advance notice.

Summary

In summary, the objectives of deregulation varied depending on the industry. In the case of the airlines, legislation was intended to increase travel opportunities for the general public and open up opportunities for all-cargo carriers like FedEx and UPS. By deregulating the industry, competition was expected to increase and result in lower passenger fares and cargo rates. The objective of deregulating motor carriers was to improve their operating efficiencies and thus reducing fuel costs, which was a major concern in the 1970s. Finally, legislation was enacted to improve railroad economic viability. Most would agree that reforms were needed at the time, although the results have not always been positive, as discussed in the next section.

Economic Impact of Deregulation

Deregulation had both a positive and negative impact on the airline industry. Existing airlines were able to make equipment changes, add seats, and reconfigure their routes to be more productive and increase aircraft utilization. The 10 "mega" airlines developed hub-and-spoke systems to route their aircraft through one or more "hub" airports. An airline generally had a dominant presence in these hubs, making it easier to control fares. For example, Delta Airlines' main hub was Atlanta; Continental Airlines' was Houston; and American Airlines' was Dallas.

There were also many airlines that filed for bankruptcy because they could not adapt to the new environment, such as Braniff and Frontier. However, multiple new airlines emerged to pick up smaller markets and the major airlines developed "feeder" carriers that brought passengers to their hubs. Eventually, through a series of mergers, the 10 mega carriers were reduced to four, which in 2021 controlled about 80% of the market.

For airline passengers, deregulation has had both positive and negative impacts. The changes have made air travel more affordable for the general public, who can travel to almost any medium-sized to large airport. Until 2020, deregulation also increased demand, meaning seats were filled at near to complete capacity; seats were also smaller and there was less legroom, increasing passenger discomfort. In 2020, the Covid-19 pandemic negatively impacted the airline industry financially, with passenger load factors falling to less than 60%. (In 2019, the load factors averaged around 83%.) In 2021, passengers began traveling again but with many restrictions. To ensure the safety of passengers and airport staff, the FAA required face coverings to be worn both inside the airport and while flying.

Deregulation had a positive effect on the air cargo markets. Similar to passenger airlines, carriers like FedEx and UPS were able to make changes to increase the utilization of their aircraft and routes. The pandemic actually had a positive impact on air cargo, with increases of 10% to 11% (Bureau of Labor Statistics, 2021).

In the long run, deregulation has benefited both motor carriers and railroads. Motor carriers initially faced severe competition from new carriers and then fallout as bankruptcy filings increased. However, deregulation enabled the remaining, more adept carriers to cut costs and improve productivity. The market has trended upward since 2000 and was valued at close to $800 billion in 2019, with most U.S. overland freight moved by truck (Mazareanu, 2020). The Staggers Act similarly enabled the railroads to reallocate resources where necessary, improve their route structures, and reduce rates. While lower rates decreased revenues, cost reductions offset lost revenue (Ellig, 2020).

Companies throughout the United States relied on the railroads for the movement of trailers (trailer on flatcar) and containers (container on flatcar) due to a shortage of truck drivers.

Federal Transportation Agencies

Established by Congress in 1966, DOT is the agency responsible overall for safety, systems, technology, and mass transit development. Led by the Secretary of Transportation, DOT's mission is to "ensure America has the safest, most efficient and modern transportation system in the world..." (Department of Transportation, 2021). As illustrated in Figure 2.3, DOT includes nine federal agencies that promote transportation. A brief description of several of those agencies follows.

Federal Aviation Administration

The FAA is primarily responsible for the safety of the aviation system. It rates and certifies pilots and airports. It is charged with regulating a program that ensures the security of civil aviation and enforces the provisions of the Hazardous Materials Transportation Act. It operates all airport towers, routes air traffic through its control towers, and develops air traffic rules.

Federal Highway Administration

The Federal Highway Administration (FHWA) partners with a variety of stakeholders—including other federal agencies, state DOTs, metro planning organizations and local public agencies—to administer its programs. These include the Highway Safety Improvement Program, the Federal Aid to Highway Program (FAHP), and the Federal Lands Highway Program. The Federal Lands Highway Program, for example, is responsible for permitting road access into and out of public lands; preparing plans and contracts; developing surveys; supervising construction; and inspecting bridges when necessary.

Federal Railroad Administration

The Federal Railroad Administration's mission is to enable a safe rail transportation system through regulation and inspection. Federal safety inspectors monitor the railroads to ensure they follow standards for operating practices

Figure 2.3 DOT organization chart

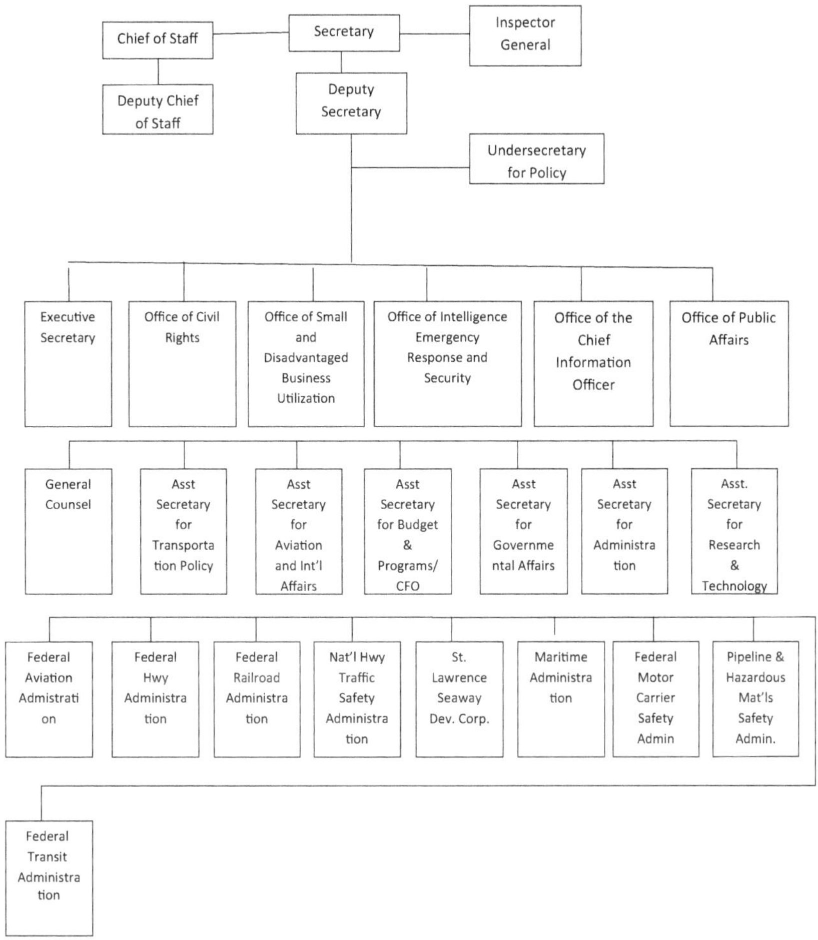

Source: DOT. www.transportation.gov/org-chart

and maintenance of tracks. It also provides educational programs to educate the public on railroad crossing safety and the dangers of trespassing on railroad property.

National Highway Traffic Safety Administration

The National Highway Traffic Safety Administration (NHTSA) is responsible for reducing deaths, injuries, and economic losses resulting from motor vehicle crashes. The NHTSA sets and enforces safety performance standards for motor vehicles and equipment. It also investigates safety defects in motor vehicles; sets and enforces fuel economy standards; helps states and local communities reduce the threat of drunk drivers; promotes the use of safety belts, child safety seats, and air bags; investigates odometer fraud; establishes and enforces vehicle anti-theft regulations; and provides consumer information on motor vehicle safety topics.

Federal Transit Administration

The Federal Transit Administration (FTA) assists in developing improved mass transportation systems for cities and communities nationwide. Through its grant programs, the FTA helps plan, build, and operate transit systems with convenience, cost, and accessibility in mind. In providing financial, technical, and planning assistance, the agency provides leadership and resources for safe and technologically advanced local transit systems, while assisting in the development of local and regional traffic reduction.

Great Lakes Saint Lawrence Seaway

Great Lakes Saint Lawrence Seaway oversees the movement of commercial and noncommercial vessels through the Saint Lawrence Seaway in cooperation with its Canadian counterpart, providing inspection of vessels, navigation aids, and traffic control. It also looks for trade opportunities that could benefit the local community.

Maritime Administration

The Maritime Administration (MARAD) assures national security and promotes the U.S. shipping industry. It works to ensure competitiveness of the U.S. shipbuilding industry through its subsidy programs for vessel operations. MARAD also works to improve U.S. participation in foreign and domestic trade.

Pipeline and Hazardous Materials Safety Administration

The Pipeline and Hazardous Material Safety Administration (PHMSA) oversees the safe movement of more than 1 million daily shipments of hazardous materials in the United States and 65% of the nation's energy that is transported by pipelines. The PHMSA is dedicated solely to ensuring the safety of hazardous materials by developing classification, handling, and packaging regulations. The Office of Pipeline Safety works to ensure that pipelines are properly designed and constructed with spill response plans in place.

Federal Motor Carrier Safety Administration

Established in 2000, the Federal Motor Carrier Safety Administration is charged with preventing commercial truck-related injuries and fatalities. Its purview includes:

- enforcing safety regulations;
- improving safety information systems;
- strengthening standards; and
- increasing safety awareness.

Conclusions

The government has been heavily involved in ensuring economically viable and safe transportation systems. Initially, the role of the government was to protect the shipper through regulation. Later, the government continued with regulation to protect various modes of transportation from competition. Today, the United States faces a largely deregulated environment, which began in the late 1970s. DOT, with its various programs, remains in place to promote private transportation to the public, regulate the safety of all modes, and ensure the continuation of U.S. infrastructure through subsidies and the construction of highways, airports, and bridges.

References

Bureau of Transportation Statistics (2021). "U.S. Airlines Carried 17% More Cargo in December 2020 than December 2019," February 17. www.bts.gov/newsroom/us-airlines-carried-17-more-cargo-december-2020-december-2019.

Department of Transportation (2021). transportation.gov.

Department of Transportation (2021). "About DOT." www.transportation.gov/about.

Ellig, J. (2020). "Forty Years after Surface Freight Deregulation," The Regulatory Review, December 14. www.theregreview.org/2020/12/14/ellig-forty-years-after-surface-freight-deregulation/.

Harberson, R. (1959). "The Transportation Act of 1958," Land Economics 35(2), 156–171.
International Maritime Organization (2021). "Introduction to IMO." www.imo.org/en/About/Pages/Default.aspx.
Mall, S. (2019). "Flashback: Interstate Trucking Under the ICC's Thumb," Freightwaves, February 8. www.freightwaves.com/news/news/economics/flashback-friday-interstate-commerce-commission-3.
Mazareanu, E. (2020). "Trucking Industry in the U.S. – Statistics and Facts," Statistica, September 11. www.statista.com/topics/4912/trucking-industry-in-the-us/#dossierSummary.
Moore, T. G. (1995). "Clearing the track: The remaining transportation regulations," Regulation, 18(2).
Sampson, R. J., Farris, M. T., & Shrock, D. L. (1985). *Domestic Transportation: Practice, Theory, and Policy.* Boston, MA: Houghton Mifflin Company.
Stanley, L. & Matthews, D. (2007). *Logistics and Transportation.* Herndon, VA: National Institute of Governmental Purchasing, Inc.
U.S. Department of Transportation Maritime Administration (2021). "The Jones Act." www.maritime.dot.gov/ports/domestic-shipping/domestic-shipping.
U.S. Department of Transportation Maritime Division (2021). "Cargo Preference." www.maritime.dot.gov/ports/cargo-preference/cargo-preference.
United States Senate (2021). "Landmark Legislation: The Pacific Railroad Act of 1862." www.senate.gov/artandhistory/history/common/generic/PacificRailwayActof1862.htm#:~:text=The%20Pacific%20Railway%20Act%2C%20which,nation's%20first%20transcontinental%20rail%20line.

Chapter 3

Mode and Carrier Selection

Introduction

The means by which items are delivered following a purchase is frequently overlooked. These could include items such as computers, office supplies, or auto parts. The focus of attention is often on the solicitation method or contract type, with issues of delivery an afterthought. The determination of the mode of transportation is an essential step in the government procurement process and thus merits consideration.

Certainly, some transportation means are more common than others in the public sector. Having goods shipped via the ground freight carrier determined by the supplier is a common approach; but there are a number of other tools available for today's government buyer, such as air freight, rail, water, and pipelines. With all of these logistical options, the public buyer is challenged with making the right determination for each particular purchase. Whether or not the delivery services should be purchased separately is another decision that must be made. Will the contract for the purchase of goods also include the transportation? Will the transportation services involve a separate agreement with another supplier? These are fundamental considerations in the procurement process.

Along with the choice of transportation mode comes the selection of the carrier that will actually transport the goods. Many companies offer both public and contracted transportation services to their clients. In most transportation

DOI: 10.4324/9781003298625-3

industries, this creates a sound, competitive environment, with the selection of the "right" carrier ultimately falling to the procurement professional. This type of challenge is one of the reasons that transportation system selection is viewed as a specialized form of procurement.

Auxiliary services also play a valuable role in transportation. These may include third-party service providers such as freight forwarders, brokers, and 3PLs. Depending on the level of expertise within an entity, as well as the staffing capacity, having a third party lend its logistics expertise can be a good investment for an organization.

Transportation Modes

Transportation is a complex industry that includes a number of modes, or types, of delivery methods. Both public and private buyers have various options available to them for transporting goods and materials. The five primary modes of transportation are:

- motor carriage;
- air cargo;
- rail freight;
- water; and
- pipeline.

Each of these modes has its own unique capabilities, with inherent advantages and disadvantages, as shown in Figure 3.1. This is followed by an overview and analysis of each mode.

Motor Carriage

The dominant mode of transportation is motor carriage, or trucking. This is a $700 billion industry that accounts for nearly 6% of all full-time jobs in the United States. The industry employs millions of drivers and moves over 70% of the country's freight (John, 2019). It consists of a large number of small motor carriers, which results in a very high level of competition. Public and private organizations use this mode extensively because of high availability, ease of accessibility, relatively fast transit times, and a generally reliable level of service. The motor carrier industry has two roughly equal segments: *for-hire carriage* and *private carriage*. For-hire carriage moved by the TL accounts for 95% of activity, with LTL accounting for the remaining 5% (Statista, 2021).

Figure 3.1 Comparison of transportation modes

Mode	Shipment types	Advantages	Disadvantages
Motor carriage	■ Parcels ■ LTL ■ TL	■ Easy accessibility ■ Reliable service ■ Fast transit times ■ Good security	■ Impacted by weather ■ Transit not always smooth ■ High shipping rates
Rail freight	■ Commodities ■ CL ■ LCL ■ Containers ■ Trailers	■ Move large volumes ■ Low cost ■ Unaffected by weather	■ Limited accessibility ■ Long transit times
Air cargo	■ Documents ■ Parcels ■ Containers	■ Fast delivery times ■ Smooth transit	■ High shipping rates ■ Limited accessibility
Water	■ Commodities ■ Equipment ■ Containers	■ Ideal for bulk material ■ Support global trade	■ Limited accessibility ■ Long transit times ■ Lower reliability
Pipeline	■ Bulk	■ Dependable transit times ■ Unaffected by weather	■ Initial investment costly ■ Limited to certain materials

The average TL delivery spans about 350 miles, with market dominance continuing up to 750 miles. Trucks move items such as raw materials, component parts, and finished goods. Trucking companies also support the rail industry, often loading their trailers onto railcars for transport. Other motor carriers include parcel delivery services such as UPS and FedEx. These privately owned carriers provide package delivery services for many government entities. Items such as repair parts and office supplies are commonly transported in this way due to competitive pricing and strong commitment to service.

The question often arises as to who is responsible for the loading and unloading of an LTL shipment. According to the National Motor Freight Classification, responsibilities are clearly spelled out in Item 58:

> *Heavy or Bulky Freight-Loading or Unloading.* When a freight container weighs less than 110 pounds, the carrier will perform both the loading and the unloading. For freight packages or pieces over 500 pounds, the consignor is required to perform the loading and the consignee the unloading. The truck driver may assist with loading or unloading upon request. When it comes to freight between 110 and 500 pounds, the driver's responsibility depends on whether the consignor

> (sender) or consignee (receiver) provides an accessible dock or ramp. Again, upon request, the truck driver may assist with the loading and unloading.
>
> (Bohman, 2002)

Within the motor carrier industry, there are four basic types of carriers (Coyle, Bardi, & Langley, 1996). The majority of industrial freight is transported by *common carriers*, which offer the transportation of goods to any shipper based on published tariffs that must be reasonable and nondiscriminatory to the shipper. Tariffs are based on a classification system, or grouping of products, based on similar transportation characteristics. *Contract carriers* are somewhat different than common carriers in that they operate under set contractual agreements with designated customers rather than the general public (although these lines have blurred since deregulation). The services can be tailored to meet the specialized needs of the shipper, providing special equipment or arranging for customized pickup and delivery schedules. *Exempt carriers* make up a third category, so called because they are exempt from economic regulation of rates and services. The marketplace determines their rates. Exempt carriers are limited to the movement of agricultural products, newspapers, livestock, and fish. The fourth category comprises *private carriers* and involves the transportation of materials with trucks and equipment owned by an agency or company. Private carriers are not "for-hire" and are exempt from federal economic regulation—for example, electrical supply houses and governments that handle their own transportation (Stanley & Matthews, 2008).

Although air freight has made significant inroads into the trucking share of transportation, trucks still account for the majority of small package shipments. In 2019 the trucking industry contributed $369 billion to GDP in the United States. Transportation services for hire accounted for $170 billion, with in-house trucking accounting for the remainder (U.S. DOT, 2020).

The future looks generally bright for this industry, with continued growth expected in the coming years. In addition, there will be consolidations of TL and LTL carriers, as well as outsourcing by private fleets. The need for qualified drivers remains a challenge for the trucking industry. In 2020 there were over 3 million truck drivers in the United States, which is less than what is needed. The diversity of drivers continues to increase, including groups that have not historically been a part of the industry. The number of African American and Hispanic drivers has increased in recent years; the same applies to women drivers and members of the LGBT community. Traditionally, women served in support or clerical roles in the trucking industry; but today they are commonly behind the wheel of big rigs, making significantly higher wages. Total Transportation reported in 2020 that women made up 19% of its driving force and it expects this number to grow. A leading provider of truck transport in Mississippi, it has found a partnership with the Women in Trucking Association to be beneficial for both employees and customers (Commendatore, 2020).

Rail Freight

There are eight large railroads, referred to as *Class I carriers*, in the United States, with more than 500 additional small operators. Class I railroads earn in excess of $266 million per year. Although Canada does not use the class system, Canadian National Railroad and Canadian Pacific Railroad would also qualify as Class I carriers.

Class I carriers account for approximately 9% of revenue generated by all modes, moving about 25% of all freight tonnage (Stanley & Matthews, 2007). Coal, grain, metallic ores, crushed stone, and glass and clay products are commodities that are commonly carried on railroads. All railroads are considered common carriers, with the legal responsibility to serve all customers at reasonable prices without discrimination.

One of the prime advantages of rail transport is the ability to move large volumes of all types of commodities over a great distance with a relatively low-cost structure. As in the trucking industry, rail shipments move in CL as well as LCL shipments. A significant disadvantage is the limited access provided by the railways, which results in the need for additional transportation modes to complete deliveries. Another disadvantage is the long transit time due to the consolidation and transfer of boxcars at yards within the rail system. However, rail service remains an extremely viable means of transportation for a variety of commodities. The reliability and dependability of rail transport are greater than for other modes, because it is generally unaffected by poor weather. For example, a snowstorm in the Midwest can easily shut down truck travel, but trains will normally continue on to their destinations.

With the trucking industry remaining one of the largest customers of rail, it will continue to be a formidable player in transportation. In the past two decades, the total miles of rail infrastructure decreased by 23%. However, total track miles in the United States still exceed 92,000, allowing trains to make dependable hauls throughout the country (U.S. DOT, 2020). Through the next decade, rail transportation will continue to benefit from growth in foreign trade, which should translate into healthy increases in rail intermodal traffic.

Air Cargo

In 2000, a total of $27 billion was spent on international and domestic air freight. That amount is still considered relatively small in the transportation market. The movement of goods through the air has certainly increased in recent years, but the relatively high cost has kept its use limited within government procurement. There are times, however, when an air shipment makes the most sense due to unforeseen inventory shortages or equipment failures. In such cases, a procurement professional would likely find the quicker delivery well worth the higher price of transportation.

As a general rule of thumb, the freight rates for air cargo are approximately twice as high as those for motor freight. However, along with the higher costs are certain advantages. Because air travel is usually much smoother than ground transportation, it is very attractive for transporting delicate equipment (Institute for Public Procurement, 2000). Another advantage is the shorter delivery times involved with air transport. A specialized repair part, for instance, can be shipped from New York to California in one day, with many commercial companies providing this service. Since typical motor carrier delivery takes several days, the option to use air freight becomes that much more attractive. With shorter lead times for products, entities can normally reduce their inventories on hand, as well as their carrying costs.

In recent years, the air transportation industry has experienced very strong growth. In 2017, the volume of freight tons transported exceeded 58 million. Companies such as UPS, FedEx and Amazon made investments in their aircraft fleet, some even converting Boeing 767 passenger aircraft to freighters (Kroll, 2017). With the global Covid-19 pandemic negatively impacting personal travel by air, the freight industry seemed to withstand the storm. In 2020, freight shipments by air declined nearly 20% globally, but revenue actually increased to $128 billion.

Water

Water transportation plays a significant role in logistics spending, accounting for over $13 billion attributed to the GDP of the United States (U.S. DOT, 2020). The majority of water transportation is undertaken by for-hire vessels. This mode is frequently used by entities located in strategic areas to move raw materials, heavy items, and low-value bulk materials. Road salt is one example of a common government commodity that is often transported by water. Water carriers—the oldest method of transportation—include barges used on inland waterways and ocean-going ships.

The costs of pickup and delivery of goods to the dockside must be included in the total cost of shipping, as these costs are not included in water freight rates. Water carriers normally base their charges on either weight or volume, depending on which results in the highest revenue for the carrier (Stanley &

Matthews, 2008). The Federal Government has been involved in improving the waterways within the United States for a long time. The U.S. Army Corps of Engineers is the agency that provides oversight and funding for river and harbor improvements (e.g., enlarging docks and deepening channels).

Waterborne commerce remains a strong force, with growth in recent years of approximately 2.6% annually. Although 2020 saw a decline in world trade due to the global pandemic (11.%), industry leaders believe water transportation will continue to play a vital role in logistics management, including in the United States (IBIS World, 2021).

Pipelines

Pipelines, referred to as the "hidden giant of American transportation," have been around since 1865, when Samuel Van Syckel constructed a five-mile oil pipeline in Pennsylvania (Wood & Johnson, 1995). Along with extensive use in the oil industry, pipelines are also used to transport other materials, such as natural gas and coal slurry. From 2000 to 2019, the total miles of oil pipeline increased by over 2%. Total gas pipeline mileage exceeded 2.5 million in 2019 (U.S. DOT, 2020).

Pipeline transit makes a significant contribution to GDP in the United States. During 2019, nearly $54 billion was attributed to this mode (U.S. DOT, 2020). Since 1977, the Federal Energy Regulatory Commission has regulated the oil pipeline industry.

The dependability of this transportation mode is extremely high when it comes to getting the product to its destination when promised. Because pipelines are virtually unaffected by the weather, they really have no equal when it comes to dependability. One disadvantage of pipeline transportation is the high cost associated with installing and maintaining piping systems. The material, labor, and equipment costs can be extensive, including such things as specialty piping, journey-level labor, pumps, and computerized flow controls. Still, pipelines continue to be a viable means of transportation in the United States, particularly in the oil and natural gas industries.

Case Study: Trans Alaska Pipeline

The Trans Alaska Pipeline System (TAPS) was one of the largest construction projects in history. Built from 1974 to 1977, the 800-mile pipeline remains an engineering marvel to this day. The pipeline is 48 inches in diameter and runs through Alaska from Prudhoe Bay to Valdez.

Owned and operated by Alyeska Pipeline Service Company, TAPS utilizes 11 pump stations and 178 gate valves to transport crude oil. During its 44-year life, the pipeline has moved more than 18 billion barrels of oil. While TAPS operates at less than full capacity, it is capable of moving 2 million barrels of oil per day.

Source: Alyeska Pipeline Services Co., www.alyeska-pipe.com/taps-facts/

The Sixth Mode of Transportation?

In recent years, both academics and practitioners have debated the inclusion of the Internet as the sixth mode of transportation. Walton (2014) notes that commerce occurs every day on the Internet, and that the delivery of purchased items often occurs virtually. For example, music or books purchased online that would traditionally be shipped via common carrier can arrive instantly through digital technology.

Supporters of this mode cite numerous benefits of the Internet as compared to traditional modes of transportation. Reduced fuel consumption, elimination of product packaging, and time savings are often cited as key benefits. Ultimately, costs can be decreased for both the supplier and the consumer. While the addition of the Internet to the five traditional modes of transportation may be a challenge for some industry leaders, it is difficult to argue that its use brings many advantages to the transportation industry.

Intermodal Carriage

Organizations often use more than one mode of transportation to move freight to its destination. Intermodal carriage—the use of two or more transportation modes to deliver goods to their ultimate destination—fills the gap (Coyle et al., 1996). This combined method of transport surfaced back in the 1800s, when the Long Island Railroad offered to carry farmers' wagons on flat cars bound for New York City (Wood & Johnson, 1995).

Intermodal service may be necessary because of the limits of each individual mode of transportation. For example, air delivery is limited to airports and requires transfer and delivery by landed modes such as rail and motor carriage. Thus, various modes can be combined to overcome their limitations while moving freight at the lowest possible cost. Motor carriage is used frequently in intermodal freight movements due to its high accessibility to destination points.

Intermodal carriage most commonly involves moving loaded trailers or containers from the shipper's facility on one type of carrier and then finishing the journey on another type of carrier. The typical surface container comes in standard sizes of 20 or 40 feet long and 8 feet wide.

Various terms have been created to describe intermodal movements of freight. For example, when shipments are moved from truck tractor to a railcar for long-haul movements, this is referred to as *piggyback*. The term *fishyback* is used when water and motor carriers ship the container; while *birdyback* refers to freight movement by air and truck. Other combinations are also possible, as shown in Figure 3.2.

In the past, transportation regulations in the United States discouraged multimodal transportation companies—those offering more than one type of transportation. Since deregulation, however, the buying market has demanded more efficient and more cost-effective transportation, which has helped to bolster the growth of intermodalism (Wood & Johnson, 1995). While carriers once offered multiple transportation modes to their customers to stay competitive, most have returned to their primary mode and added other services. UPS and FedEx are two notable exceptions, each with a fleet of aircraft and trucks. Partnerships between motor carriers, railroads, or motor carriers and railroads are more commonly negotiated today, to improve service and costs for shippers. For example, the Burlington Northern and Santa Fe Railway Company (BNSF) and the Norfolk Southern Railway Company offer coast-to-coast CL service for temperature-controlled commodities from the Washington State cities of Seattle, Tacoma, Yakima, and Pasco to the Midwest, Northeast, and Southeast (www.bnsf.com). Intermodal marketing companies have also been created, acting as intermediaries to solicit intermodal traffic for the railroads.

Figure 3.2 Intermodal options

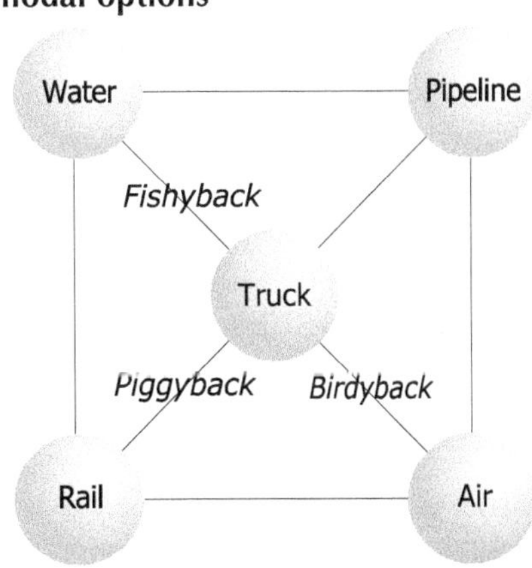

With options for integrating multiple modes and providing maximum flexibility, intermodal transportation will continue to benefit global markets and distribution systems. It requires a broader knowledge of transportation processes within the supply chain, as it focuses on a holistic view of transportation (DeWitt & Clinger, 2000).

Carrier Selection

According to Leenders and Flynn (1995), choosing the right supplier can help ensure operational success for an organization. This is certainly the case when purchasing goods, but it can be just as important when it comes to determining how those same goods will be transported to their final destination. While the initial determination made by an entity may very well be mode of delivery, the choice of carrier will certainly be next. It is not difficult to see how important quality and timely goods are to an entity—particularly when one considers the seven "Rights" of customer satisfaction:

- the Right product;
- delivered to the Right place;
- at the Right time;
- in the Right condition;
- in the Right quantity;
- at the Right cost;
- to the Right customer.

(Kuglin, 1998)

The importance of quality, accuracy, and timeliness in the delivery of goods is apparent. These factors influence which carrier the procurement professional ultimately selects.

Who Manages the Transportation Decision?

A key consideration for public procurement professionals at all levels is whether to buy transportation and delivery services separate from the goods purchase itself. The predominant trend within the public arena is to shift the burden of carrier selection to the supplier. With a goods contract that includes delivery (often in the form of a purchase order), the supplier is responsible for determining which carrier will be used.

Even though many government purchases require the supplier to handle carrier selection, in many instances it can be beneficial to contract separately for transportation. Many entities handle the outbound shipping of goods and equipment from their own facilities and contract directly with carriers to transport them. For example, when a water treatment facility needs to ship specialized control equipment to the equipment manufacturer for repair or upgrade, to ensure the quality transportation of such critical equipment, the entity may likely have a contract already in place with a carrier. The carrier will pick up the equipment at the specified location and then transport it to the manufacturer's facility. Once the necessary repairs are completed, the entity will hire the carrier to bring the equipment back for its scheduled installation. This approach can also be viable for incoming freight. Rather than relying on an unknown carrier selected by the supplier, an entity may wish to contract with its own carrier. This offers the entity more control and oversight during the transportation process, and may even result in a lower cost.

Some may feel that it is easier to simply rely on the supplier to select the carrier. This often takes less entity staff time and energy, and will likely have favorable results. When a time- critical shipment is needed, most organizations would rather be in control of carrier delivery. Suppliers also determine the cost of transportation, which may not always be to the entity's benefit. Purchasing and supply managers are in the best position to work with their suppliers to keep transportation costs down (Pinkerton & Marien, 1997).

If procurement professionals decide to contract for transportation services, they will face many of the same issues encountered with other types of services. A determination must be made as to which procurement method will be employed. Traditionally, many government services are awarded through an invitation for bids (IFB) process. This solicitation method sets out minimum requirements, with the contract usually going to the bidder providing the lowest price. A request for proposals (RFP) process is another option for procurement professionals. An RFP will take into account other aspects of the proposal that the entity considers of value. These can include service quality, corporate experience, finance stability, past performance, and sustainability.

In contracting for services, including transportation, procurement professionals have several options. Depending upon the contracting rules of the entity, direct negotiations may be appropriate and allowable. As in other procurements, it is the procurement professional's responsibility to help determine the most appropriate means of purchasing. By keeping abreast of current trends and methods, one can draw on the best solution or practice for a given situation. No single procurement method will fit every need. According to the National Association of State Procurement Officials (NASPO) (2001),

"It must be recognized that, while the purchase of services requires innovative methods of acquiring quality services at a reasonable price, traditional procurement strategies are amenable to the process" (p. 74).

The current process will likely accommodate techniques for saving money. Regardless of the procurement and contract type utilized, transportation contracts give carriers the opportunity to secure a large volume of business from an entity. Such opportunities normally result in very favorable offers from the carrier community. Additionally, long-term agreements with multi-year options can provide an opportunity for a carrier to become a strategic partner of the entity. Once the contract is executed and the business relationship is formally established, the entity can utilize the carrier as the need arises. Sound contract documents, frequent communications, and effective contract administration can all contribute to a favorable partnership for both parties. Similar agreements can also be made with third-party providers of transportation services. When an entity contracts with a freight forwarder or broker, such contractors can provide whatever transportation mode is needed, which offers the buyer greater flexibility.

Logistics Support Services

Most organizations, including state and local governments, utilize outside logistics services to supplement their own workforce. Such efforts allow procurement professionals to fulfill the service delivery needs of their respective entities. A critical part of their role is to coordinate the flow of goods and services throughout the entity and in support of its objectives. Whether the services are performed internally or externally may be of no consequence to an end user. If the traffic signal equipment arrives at the project site on time, the needs of the engineer overseeing the intersection project have been met. It is this type of operational contribution that procurement professionals need to concentrate on when evaluating their role within the entity. The outside, auxiliary services can take on a variety of forms.

Third-Party Logistics Providers

3PLs are independent companies that design, implement, or manage an organization's supply chain logistics needs. A key difference between a 3PL and a typical transportation service provider is that the 3PL's value is based on information and knowledge, as opposed to simply providing the same service at a lower cost (Konezny & Beskow, 1999). This is a growing area for organizations of all types. In 2019, the use of 3PLs exceeded $1 trillion and it is estimated to increase by at least 9% by 2026 (Mayer, 2020).

Figure 3.3 Outsourced logistics services

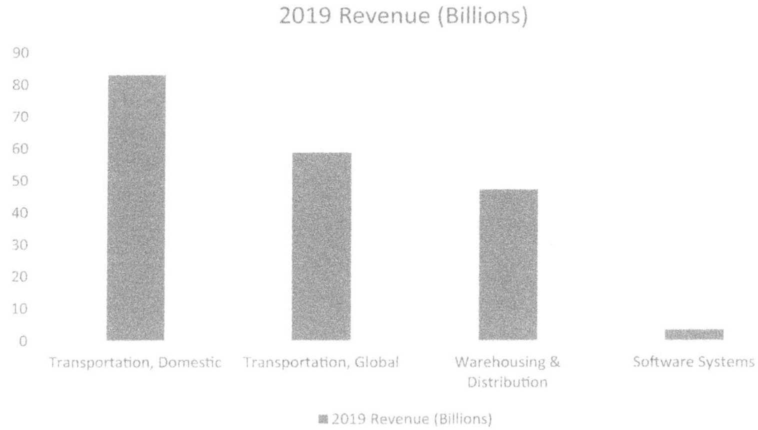

Adapted from Armstrong, E. (2021). "What is Outsourced Logistics? Everything you need to know about using 3PLs," Coyote a UPS Company. www.coyote.com.

While there may be different levels of use and integration of 3PLs within an entity, some of the most common functions are presented in Figure 3.3 Some of the performance standards that an entity might use with these providers are similar to its own operations. Factors such as inventory accuracy, turnaround time, client satisfaction, and on-time deliveries are all important.

In addition to many organizations that currently use 3PLs, others will likely look to consider them in the future. Inbound and outbound transportation, warehousing, and distribution seem to be the areas in which 3PLs are most commonly used, but other functions—such as customer service and information technology—appear to be gaining ground. This means that 3PLs must be able to provide a wide array of services to meet this demand, both today and in the future. This includes the use of leading technology in their operations, expertise with foreign markets, and a commitment to customer service.

It should be added that a key to successfully working with 3PLs is maintaining a sound relationship with the provider. Developing a sound contractual agreement and a bond of mutual trust can play well for both parties. While it may likely be the financial or executive powers that recognize the need for a 3PL, the entity will certainly rely on the procurement and supply chain professional when it comes to implementation.

4PLs and 5PLs

Within the transportation industry, a 3PL is considered to have advanced to a 4PL when it manages other logistics, resources, and technology to enhance the level of service it offers. A 4PL can increase its capacity and expand its geographic service area as part of a more complete transportation solution (Mayer, 2020). It can also assume more management functions for a customer, including sourcing, budgeting, and distribution.

While a newer concept in transportation management, the use of 5Pls is becoming more and more common. These providers focus on managing not just supply chains, but also supply chain networks. Therefore, a 5PL provides a high level of logistical services to multiple customers. It typically has a great deal of expertise in e-commerce support and system integration.

Freight Forwarders

Freight forwarders provide a valuable service by providing transportation to firms with LCL lots. These smaller shipments are combined with other such shipments to make a full load and then transported at the CL rate. Freight forward shipments normally move more quickly than ordinary LCL shipments if the traveling distance is over 300 miles. The rates are quite competitive. In nearly all cases, freight forwarder rates are at least as low as LCL and LTL rates. On longer hauls, they can be significantly lower (NIGP, 2010).

Air freight forwarders operate in a similar manner to the truck and rail companies. Many offer a combination of surface and air transport for their shipments, which can result in a great deal of flexibility for their customers. Air freight forwarders can use their ground transportation carriers to offset the overall shipping costs, making this less expensive than direct air service.

Brokers

Freight brokers are similar to forwarders, in that they can provide transportation to firms with LCL and LTL shipping needs. The broker is an individual or firm that acts as an intermediary between a buyer and a seller (Hinkelman, 2000). Brokers are experts within the transportation industry and are usually very well connected. They broker the shipments and coordinate the transportation with one or more carriers, ensuring that the goods end up at the right place at the right time. Serving as an agent to both parties (buyer and seller), the broker normally works on a commission basis. Sometimes the term "broker" may not be viewed favorably within the public sector, as it is not actually the firm "doing the work." However, in the logistics arena, brokers can provide a valuable service to the government, offering a level of shipping expertise that can benefit the entity on an as-needed basis, as well as saving the entity transportation costs.

Designing a Transportation Program

Historically, the public sector has left the transportation decision to the supplier. That is, whichever supplier earns the contract or purchase calls the shots on how the goods are delivered. However, some entities are seeing the benefits of taking more control of freight movements.

There are many things for a procurement and supply chain professional to consider when establishing a transportation program. Once it is determined that purchasing and supply will control inbound transportation, efforts should be coordinated with the supplier. Initially, suppliers may be resistant to this change in business practice, so it is important to gain their cooperation. Additionally, suppliers can offer important contacts in the transportation industry that will be needed to coordinate freight movements from their facility to the final destination.

A team effort is also important to assure success, no matter how big or small the entity may be. Key members of the team should include transportation and distribution, inventory management, quality assurance, and accounting—with procurement and supply management taking the lead.

Carrier Selection Checklist

There are many things to consider when selecting a transportation carrier. Using the right carrier to deliver the needed goods to the right location continues to be an extremely important axiom. The condition of the goods and the timing of delivery are a direct reflection on the procurement department. The following list presents some key issues to consider during carrier selection:

- What types of goods will be moved?
- What is the best mode of transportation? Are multiple modes required?
- What are the entity's shipping points and "traffic lanes" with the highest volumes?
- What are the delivery requirements?
- What is the best method of solicitation (e.g., IFB, RFP, negotiation)?
- What criteria will be used for selection (e.g., cost, financial stability, past performance, service capacity)?
- Who owns the goods during transit and who is responsible for claims?
- What are the standards of operation for the contractor?
- How are billings and payments handled?
- Will assignment of the agreement to another party be allowed?
- Is the contract renewable for additional terms?

- How are acts of God (*force majeure*), such as weather delays, dealt with?
- What constitutes a contract breach and what is the result?
- What are the remedies for disputes between the parties?

This list offers some important points to consider for procurement professionals responsible for transportation services; however, it is certainly not exhaustive. Much discussion and collaboration with client departments should occur when selecting a carrier to fulfill an entity's transportation needs. Additionally, it may be necessary to outsource some of the transportation functions to a third party, particularly if staffing is limited. 3PLs still allow purchasing and supply control of the transportation decision, but offer their expertise and a variety of options and services.

Delivery Terms

There are numerous types of shipping terms, with each term identifying certain rights and responsibilities of both the buyer and seller. Issues like carrier selection, routing, and the transfer of title are all part of these terms. The subject of ownership is important, particularly if the goods are lost or damaged in transit. Whichever party owns the goods, in accordance with the freight terms, is responsible for filing any damage claims.

The term *FOB* indicates that the price for freight includes delivery at the seller's expense to some specified point. The terms *destination* and *point of origin* describe a specific point and the responsibilities of the buyer and seller. *Point of origin* means that the title and control are transferred to the buyer, along with any risks of transportation, once the carrier signs the bill of lading. The buyer must also file any claims for loss or damage. However, routing of the shipment is at the discretion of the buyer. *Destination* indicates that the seller owns and controls the freight until it is delivered to the buyer and the contract for carriage is concluded. The seller takes responsibility for selecting the carrier and assumes all responsibility for any risks of transportation. The seller also files any claims for loss or damage. Several terms are used to describe payment terms. Figure 3.4 provides a summary of shipping options.

The most common delivery term is the requirement for *FOB Destination, Freight Prepaid and Allowed* within the entity's solicitation documents. In such instances, the selected supplier handles all aspects of product delivery, with the entity taking ownership upon delivery (Stanley & Matthews, 2002). In situations where the FOB term is silent, or is not addressed in the contract, *FOB Origin* applies as far as the passage of title in accordance with the Uniform Commercial Code.

Figure 3.4 FOB shipping terms

Freight terms	*Customer takes title of goods*	*Customer responsibilities*	*Supplier responsibilities*
FOB Point of Origin, Freight Collect	At point of origin or factory	Pays freight, bears freight charges,* owns goods in transit, files claims for loss or damage	
FOB Point of Origin, Freight Prepaid and Allowed	At point of origin or factory	Owns goods in transit, files claims	Pays freight, bears freight charges
FOB Point of Origin, Freight Prepaid and Added	At point of origin or factory	Bears freight charges, owns goods in transit, files claims	Pays freight, adds freight to invoice
FOB Destination, Freight Collect	At destination	Pays freight, bears freight charges	Owns goods in transit, files claims
FOB Destination, Freight Prepaid and Added	At destination	Bears freight charges	Pays freight, adds freight to invoice, owns goods in transit, files claims
FOB Destination, Freight Prepaid and Allowed	At destination		Pays freight, bears freight charges, owns goods in transit, files claims

Source: National Institute of Governmental Purchasing, Inc. (2004). *Sourcing in the Public Sector.* Herndon, VA: NIGP.

If an entity chooses to manage the transportation function, another option is *FOB Point of Origin*, with the option of *Freight Collect* or *Freight Prepaid and Added.* These terms should be used when it can be determined that there will be cost savings because actual freight charges are less than those built into the cost of goods purchased. Sometimes, having the purchasing entity make arrangements for the shipment of large and bulky items requiring use of an entire freight car or a full truck could result in significant savings. Examples include rolls of paper for large print jobs and road salt during the winter. An entity may also wish to deal exclusively with one carrier for all of its shipping needs. Possessing a good working knowledge of the delivery terms and knowing how to apply this appropriately when dealing with carriers can lead to an overall reduction in an entity's freight costs (Mankin, 1997).

Tariffs

Tariffs are published schedules of a carrier's rates. The transportation industry is particularly competitive today, not only within a particular mode but between modes. It is important to understand the rate structure offered by each carrier for each mode. Today, tariffs are often provided on a carrier's website. Carriers frequently offer more than one rate tariff, as well as a rules tariff and a liability tariff.

Tracing Shipments

It may be necessary to locate a shipment that is in transit and still under the control of the carrier. Today, most tracking systems are automated and available online using satellite technology. Information that may be needed to track a shipment includes:

- shipment origin;
- destination;
- date shipped;
- freight bill number; and
- a description of the goods.

Freight Invoices

A freight bill should never be paid until it has been audited. If in-house staff are not available to review bills, preferably before they are paid, special auditing firms are available that charge a commission on any savings from overcharges. Organizations have up to six months to audit freight bills. Overcharging may occur for a number of reasons, including:

- incorrect classification;
- rate calculation mistakes;
- incorrect FOB terms;
- incorrect routing;
- poor delivery;

- incorrect packaging; and
- miscellaneous additional charges that are not justifiable.

Carrier Performance

The carrier's performance should be reviewed periodically, as it is providing services on behalf of the entity and therefore reflects on the entity. Carriers may provide their own report card with information on shipment and delivery dates. There are multiple measures that can be applied, including:

- billing accuracy;
- frequency of claims;
- delivery performance;
- rate negotiations;
- technology offered;
- equipment; and
- post-evaluation performance.

Whichever performance metrics are to be used with a carrier, it is imperative they are addressed in the contract. In addition to specific services and cost structures, metrics that address service levels and reliability are essential (Mangan and Lalwani, 2016).

Conclusions

There are several modes of transportation that are available to the government. While some are more commonly used than others, they all have their niche in the world of transportation. Whether through truck freight, air shipment, water, railway, or pipelines, the public sector must have its goods transferred. Each type of transportation mode has its own advantages and disadvantages. While motor carriage is extremely flexible and affordable, after examining all costs and factors involved, the best decision in a given situation may be to use next-day air transport. Procurement professionals can make the right decisions for their entities only by knowing all of the options available and the nuances of each. In addition to the five traditional modes, digital product delivery via the Internet should be a viable option. There should be many considerations when selecting a carrier. Securing a company that is dependable and accountable can prove to be invaluable. Careful attention should be given to the procurement method employed as well as the carrier selection itself.

Contracting for logistics support services can be a valuable venture for the government. Third-party logistics providers that can perform functions such as warehousing and distribution can assist small and large entities alike. It may be time to consider outside expertise to supplement the public workforce, particularly with today's shrinking budgets. Even if shipping services are needed on an infrequent basis, using service providers such as freight forwarders and brokers can make a lot of sense. Research supports the fact that more and more areas are being considered for outsourcing, so it is time to stay current on which tasks may prove beneficial from outsourcing possibilities. Whenever public policy dictates the use of such third-party providers, the procurement professional will be the leader in integrating these services into entity operations. With continued reliance on transportation partners, 4PLs and 5PLs can be considered along with 3PLs.

The area of transportation may have been historically overlooked and undervalued, but it has truly evolved into a critical component of government procurement. While the purchase of the right goods and materials is crucial, so too is ensuring that those goods arrive at their proper destination when they are needed. Transportation has played a significant role in the economic development of the United States and continues to be a key element of the national economy. As procurement professionals interact with these transportation carriers, they also become a part of this important industry. What does the future hold? Most experts feel that changes will occur but that transportation will remain a strong and specialized field. With the expected turnover of motor carriers, consolidation of express mail firms, and increased use of e-commerce, procurement professionals will need to adapt to remain successful in the public sector.

References

Bohman, R. (2002). "Who's responsible for loading or unloading the freight?" Logistics Management, August.

Commendatore, C. (2020). "Diversity and Inclusion in Trucking," American Trucker, November 9. www.trucker.com.

Coyle, J. J., Bardi, E. J., & Langley, C. J., Jr. (1996). *The Management of Business Logistics*. St. Paul, MN: West Publishing Company.

DeWitt, D., & Clinger, J. (2000). *Intermodal Freight Transportation*. Millennium Paper, Transportation Research Board Committee on Intermodal Freight Transportation. Washington, DC: National Academy Press.

Duffy, R. J. (1999). "Logistics: A custom link," Purchasing Today, 10(3), March.

Ernst & Young (1999). *Third-Party Logistics: Views from the Customers*. Ernst & Young, Fourth Annual Study. Knoxville, TN: University of Tennessee.

Hinkelman, E. G. (2000). *Dictionary of International Trade* (4th ed.). Novato, CA: World Trade Press.
IBIS World (2021). "Industry Research Reports, Global Deep Sea, Coastal & Inland Water Transportation Industry," January 29. www.ibisworld.com.
John, S. (2019). "11 incredible facts about the $700 billion US trucking industry," Markets Insider. www.markets.businessinsider.com
Konezny G. P., & Beskow, M. J. (1999). *Third Party Logistics: Improving Global Supply Chain Performance*. Minneapolis, MN: Piper Jaffray Equity Research.
Kuglin, F. A. (1998). *Customer Centered Supply Chain Management*. New York: AMACOM, American Management Association.
Leenders, M. R., & Flynn, A. E. (1995). *Value-Driven Purchasing*. New York: National Association of Purchasing Management and Irwin Professional Publishing.
Mangan, J. & Lalwani, C. (2016). *Global Logistics and Supply Chain Management*. Chichester, UK: Wiley & Sons.
Mankin, R. T. (1997). "Understanding the ins and outs of carrier terms," Purchasing Today, 36, July.
Mayer, M. (2020). "3PL vs. 4PL vs. 5PL – Here's the Difference," Food Logistics, Transportation, July 29. www.sdce.com
Mazareanu, E. (2021). "Worldwide revenue of cargo airlines from 2004 to 2021, Transportation & Logistics, Aviation," Statista. www.statista.com.
McGinnis, M. A. (1990). "The relative importance of cost and service in freight transportation choice: Before and after deregulation," Transportation Journal, 12–19.
National Association of State Procurement Officials (NASPO). (2001). *State and Local Government Purchasing Principles and Practices*. Lexington, KY: NASPO.
National Institute of Governmental Purchasing, Inc. (NIGP) (2004). *Sourcing in the Public Sector*. Herndon, VA: NIGP.
Pinkerton, R. L., & Marien, E. J. (1997). "The fundamentals of inbound transportation," NAPM InfoEdge, 2(8), April.
Stanley, L.L. & Matthews, D.L. (2007). *Logistics and Transportation: Delivering Greater Savings and Service Options to the Community*. Herndon, VA: Institute for Public Procurement.
Stanley, L. L., & Matthews, D. L. (2003). "Logistics and transportation," *Encyclopedia of Public Administration and Public Policy*. New York: Dekker Encyclopedias, Taylor and Francis Books.
Stanley, L.L. & Matthews, D.L. (2008). *Effective Supply Management Performance*. Tempe, AZ: Institute for Supply Management.
Walton, R. O. (2014). "The 6th Mode of Transportation," Journal of Transportation Management, 5(1).
WEFA-DRI. (2001a). *Air Transportation Industry Yearbook 2001/2002*. New York: WEFA-DRI.
WEFA-DRI. (2001b). *Railroad Transportation Industry Yearbook 2001/2002*. New York: WEFA-DRI.
WEFA-DRI. (2001c). *Truck Transportation Industry Yearbook 2001/2002*. New York: WEFA-DRI.

WEFA-DRI. (2001d). *Water Transportation Industry Yearbook 2001/2002.* New York: WEFA-DRI.

Wood, D. F., & Johnson, J. C. (1995) *Contemporary Transportation* (5th ed.). Upper Saddle River, NJ: Prentice Hall.

Chapter 4

Costs of Transportation

Introduction

While often overlooked or simply left to the supplier, managing the costs of a transportation service is important to Procurement. Freight costs accounted for 7.3% of GDP in 2019, and have ranged from 7.3% to 7.9% since 2010, indicating a significant portion of supply chain costs can be attributed to transportation (Gilmore, 2020). Transportation costs also can account for about 10% of the price of a product (Rodrigue and Notteboom, 2020). Procurement often allocates the responsibility for transportation to the supplier. However, oftentimes the supplier can negotiate a volume discount with the carrier but charge full rate to Procurement as part of the purchase price. This creates an additional profit for the supplier. Thus, it is important to be able to estimate what portion of an invoice can be attributed to transportation. In other words, it is prudent to delve deeper into the cost to purchase transportation separately from the price of the supplier's products. This involves gaining a better understanding of how carriers set their rates. With knowledge in hand, Procurement can determine whether it would be better to negotiate directly with the carrier or leave that responsibility with the supplier.

This chapter provides a basis for understanding carrier costs and how they are used to determine transportation rates. It also provides some examples of services carriers provide beyond basic transportation. Lastly, it describes two analytical methods that can be used to make the transportation decision based on lowest overall costs.

DOI: 10.4324/9781003298625-4

Costing Transportation: The Carrier's Perspective

Carriers evaluate their operating costs for a number of reasons. For example, they look at their costs to create or change their transportation network so it will be the most profitable but also minimize costs. They also evaluate their costs when setting rates, which can be used as a basis to negotiate with the shipper. This process involves cost allocation. Costs can be used to determine whether to launch a new service or discontinue an existing service. Aggregated costs also can be used to develop a strategic plan or make a decision about a procurement or merger with another carrier.

At first glance, it might seem simple to allocate costs into specific categories, but in actuality it can be quite difficult. In fact, costs often can be assigned to more than one category. Standard cost terms (direct labor plus direct materials) used for accounting purposes also can be ambiguous. Standard costs are, theoretically, the costs to perform the transportation service under normal conditions. However, operating conditions can change, which can increase or reduce costs and affect standard costs. Lastly, new technologies can improve operating efficiencies. As a result, costs need to be evaluated periodically and adjusted to reflect current conditions, and may result in price increases or decreases. The following section discusses the cost categories commonly used by carriers to establish rates.

Cost Categories

From an economics standpoint, there are several categories of costs related to transportation. *Fixed costs* are those costs that do not change when there is a change in output—and remain constant regardless of the level of activity. For example, airlines make a significant investment in aircraft; motor carriers own a fleet of trucks; and railroads purchase railcars and terminals. Pipelines and railroads are classified as fixed-cost modes because of significant investments in their path of travel.

Variable costs are those costs that change as the level of output changes. Fuel costs, wages, and maintenance costs are all examples of variable costs. Airlines, water carriers, and motor carriers incur a large proportion of variable costs, such as fuel, maintenance, and labor. Airlines and water carriers also pay user fees because they do not own their travel path. Instead, cities own the airports and ports used by these carriers (Bloomberg et al., 2001).

All fixed costs eventually become variable since those purchases are considered to be long-term assets that will have to be replaced at some point in time.

For example, airlines periodically replace older aircraft. In 2021, Southwest Airlines secured a firm order for 100 Boeing 737 MAXs to replace its smaller, less fuel-efficient Boeing 737–700s (Koenig, 2021).

Overhead costs have elements of both fixed and variable costs. Examples include office equipment, support staff, and insurance. They are necessary for operating the organization but cannot be tied specifically to output. However, these costs can be managed to adjust for changes in demand.

Joint costs occur when a cost will result in the production of more than one product. These could also be categorized as *shared costs*. For example, if BNSF Railway provides rail movement from Kansas City to Houston, there might be the possibility of backhaul service or additional service to another destination—say, Brownsville, Texas. This means that the cost that was originally considered to apply directly to the trip from Kansas City to Houston could now also apply to another trip, such as the backhaul from Houston to Brownsville. Both variable and fixed costs also can be categorized as joint costs. All modes of transportation incur joint costs to some extent.

Common costs also are shared costs because they cannot be directly associated with a particular activity or activities. These costs are encountered by all modes of transportation. For example, ABC Trucking, a hypothetical trucking firm, is moving goods from Seattle to San Francisco. The truck contains five separate shipments and breaks down in transit. How should the cost of repairs be allocated? Repairs are a common cost, in that they must be shared by all of those using the truck. These costs could be compared to overhead costs. Should they be shared by weight, cubic space, or both? This is a question that has no clear answer but must be answered for accounting purposes.

Opportunity cost is the "loss of potential gain from other alternatives when one alternative is chosen" (NIGP Dictionary, 2021). The underlying implication is that resources are limited, so the entity should choose the option that results in the greatest return. For example, a trucking firm may give up a particular route in exchange for an alternative route because the return is better. While expenses for the existing route will be saved (e.g., wages, fuel), costs will still accrue for the new option. Both revenue and costs will need to be analyzed to make a final decision.

Relationship between Demand and Transportation Costs

Transportation carriers must review other factors when pricing their services. The demand of one shipper, known as *disaggregate demand*, versus the demand from all shippers, known as *aggregate demand*, is one consideration.

For example, if Union Pacific Railroad has a 100-car railcar movement from Salt Lake City to Denver, each car may be carrying a different commodity with a different origin, a different destination, and different demand characteristics. Some cars may carry coal, others automobiles, and still others a mix of products. The cost of one movement of 100 railcars is the same, but pricing will vary depending on demand for each product. The *elasticity of demand* for different products also affects the rates carriers can charge.

The elasticity of demand related to transportation has three important components. The first is actual demand for the commodity or final product. If the demand for this item is *elastic*, or sensitive to price changes, then demand for the transportation of this item will also be elastic. The elasticity of demand for transportation is frequently dependent upon the ratio of transportation charges to the final product price. However, demand for the same commodity may vary from city to city. For example, companies located in San Antonio may be willing to pay $5.50 for a bushel of corn, while companies located in Phoenix may be willing to pay $5.75 per bushel. Therefore, a middleman should be willing to pay up to $0.25 per bushel to move the corn to Denver. This is known as the spread in price between two locations.

Second, if demand for a product/commodity is *inelastic*—that is, demand is not sensitive to price changes or demand is somewhat fixed in quantity—then transportation charges are considered an input to the inelasticity of demand. These products and services typically are necessities. For example, the demand for tanker ships is considered inelastic because they are needed to support petroleum supply chain networks; and the demand for petroleum products is considered inelastic because the demand for tanker ships is inelastic.

The third element is the *time elasticity* of transportation. An investment in purchased products includes opportunity costs incurred while in transit. The product is not available for use until it is received and money has been allocated for the purchase through a purchase order that cannot be used for any other purposes. At times, shippers are willing to pay more to reduce freight time and gain access to that product more quickly—for example, by using air versus truck or rail. Perishable products such as food for cafeterias are particularly sensitive to transit times. Shippers lose potential sales if food is less than fresh upon arrival as a result of longer transit time and, therefore, are willing to pay more in transportation costs.

Basis for Determining Transportation Rates

Theoretically, carriers examine two factors to establish their rates, as shown in Figure 4.1.

Figure 4.1 Factors affecting rates

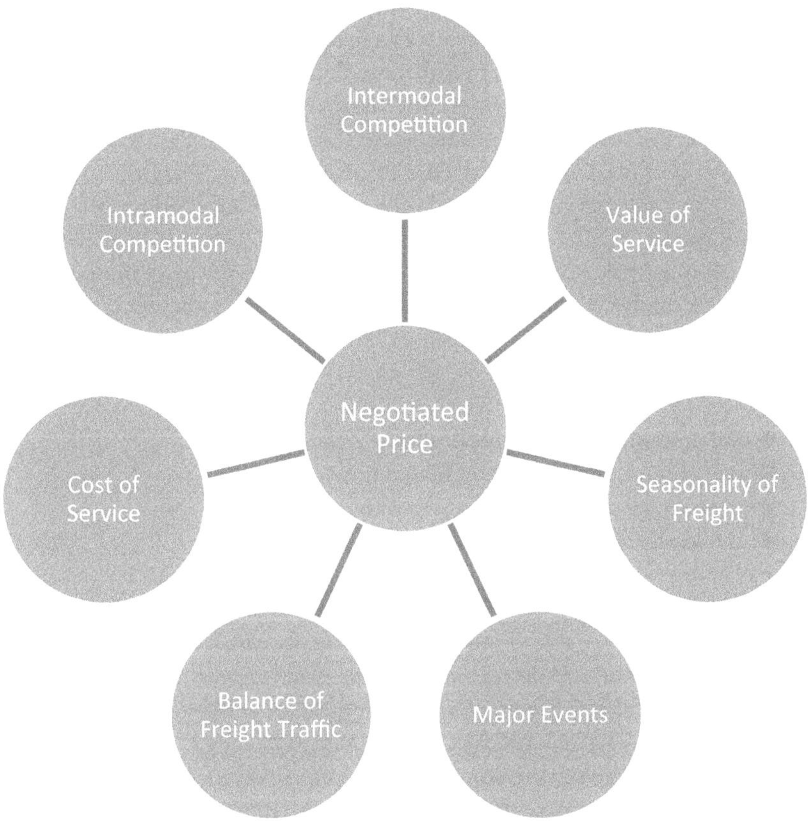

- the actual cost of providing their service(s), or *cost of service*; and
- the value of their services to the shipper, or *value of service*.

(Novack et al, 2018)

The cost-of-service approach takes a supply side view and sets the "floor" or baseline for rates. Ideally, a particular rate would cover the fixed and variable costs of providing movement of those goods plus some additional margin for profit (Grant et al., 2005). However, in some instances, a carrier might simply try to recover its fixed costs. Some of these fixed expenses include staff salaries, insurance, and lease payments. At the upper end, a carrier would attempt to recover the full cost of providing the service. Somewhere in between, carriers may charge an average of their variable and fixed, or total costs.

The difficulty in this approach lies in accurately identifying the fixed and variable costs and then determining a method of allocating a portion of their fixed costs to each shipment. Carriers also incur common and joint costs when they consolidate shipments of two or more shippers into one movement, thus making it more difficult to determine fixed and variable costs. In practice, determining the cost of service is frequently used for low-value products with thin profit margins. Carriers make use of cross-subsidies, charging rates based on fixed costs for one product and higher rates on other products, to recoup the total costs.

Carriers are more likely to charge based on the *value of service* provided, or what the traffic will allow. This method goes back to the demand side of pricing; thus, rates will vary by product based on several factors. These could include:

- the amount of competition within a mode;
- the amount of competition between modes;
- the balance of freight traffic in and out of a market; and
- the seasonality of a product movement.

Other variables also are factored into the rate equation. The distance of a movement is one variable. Longer hauls generally result in higher transportation rates but are not always proportional. Carriers also may offer *blanket rates* that cover all points within a geographical area. Blanket rates often are used in situations where a product is being shipped a long distance, and originates in one geographical region and is then unloaded in another region. For example, produce from central California (one region) is often shipped to the East Coast (another region) using a blanket rate. The U.S. Postal Service also charge blanket rates to ship packages. Areas are grouped using zip codes, known as *zones*. Rates are calculated based on the originating and destination zones.

Carriers also factor in the weight of the movement. Rates are quoted in cents per hundredweight (cwt), which is determined by dividing the actual weight in pounds by 100. Additionally, carriers often offer discounts for shipping in large quantities. For example, railroads will charge less per cwt for shipping full CLs versus LCL. Similarly, motor carriers will charge less per cwt if a shipper is moving full TLs rather than LTL. The cost differential can be attributed to the additional time and labor involved in consolidating multiple shipments because of additional stops and more frequent unloading. The dollar value of the product will influence rates charged. As dollar values increase, transportation costs tend to increase because there is a greater chance of damage—that is, a greater risk in moving higher-dollar items, resulting in higher insurance costs. The transportation company will have to pay more to reimburse the shipper should damage or loss occur. For example, a shipment of valuable paintings will cost the shipper more than a shipment of patio furniture due to the difference in value.

The density of a product, or weight/space ratio, can impact carrier rates. The greater the density, the lower the transportation costs. For example, the movement of boxed furniture, considered to have a high density, would result in lower rates than non-stackable baskets.

Carriers must factor in the risk of damage to a product. The greater chance of damage, such as in the case of breakables or oddly shaped items, the higher the transportation costs. Expensive glassware and wine bottles are examples of items with a higher risk of damage in transit.

Special handling is another consideration. Products requiring refrigeration, heating, or special stops during transit will result in higher transportation costs. For example, in 2021 the Covid-19 vaccination manufactured by Pfizer-BioNTech had a short shelf life and had to be shipped in special thermal shipping containers using dry ice. To meet these restrictive product conditions, the manufacturer contracted for air transportation, the most expensive mode, to keep the vaccine fresh (Pfizer, 2021).

Stowability, or cube utilization, is the degree to which a product fills available space within a boxcar, trailer, container, or the belly of an aircraft. Easier stowability results in lower rates. Petroleum products, for example, are easily stowed, while autos and machinery are not.

Finally, the extent of government regulation will have an impact on rates. Factors such as safety requirements, regulations on the movement of hazardous materials, and labor laws, to mention a few, all add costs to transportation movements and are factored into the rates charged.

Specific Pricing Issues

An examination of some of the basics of transportation costs and pricing leads to the various ways that carriers charge for services. Understanding the types of pricing structures prevalent in the marketplace is essential to properly apply them to a particular purchase or procurement for an entity.

Class Rates

It is important that shippers understand how LTL motor carriers price their shipments, which can seem complicated. Most commodities are priced based on *density*, or pounds per cubic foot. Rates based on density are considered the fairest way to price shipments. There are literally thousands of products and commodities that can be shipped. Since it is not feasible to establish a separate rate for every good that is transported, carriers may establish their own rates based on density alone or use the classification book published by the National Motor Freight Traffic Association Inc. (NMFTA), which combines commodities together in common categories or *classes*. The NMFTA is a Virginia-based nonprofit organization with members that operate intrastate, interstate, and globally, and is the primary classification body within the motor carrier industry. Each class of items has an assigned number, shown in Figure 4.2, which increases as

Figure 4.2 Freight classification table examples

Density (Pounds/cubic feet)	*Example*	*Class*
<1	Ping pong balls	500
⋮		⋮
4-5	Mattresses	200
⋮		⋮
8-9	Cabinets	110
⋮		⋮
15-22.5	Boxed paper	65
⋮		⋮
>35 but <50	Hardwood flooring	55
⋮		⋮
50	Bolts	50

Source: National Motor Freight Transportation Association. www.nmfta.org.

transportation of the commodity becomes more difficult. Motor carriers can use this classification system to apply a rate to an item within the specific class.

For example, shipping an item in Class 400 (i.e., not dense at all) might cost the shipper $0.45 per pound, while an item in Class 60 (fairly dense) might cost the shipper $0.15 per pound. In 2021, most carriers set their rates using the NMFTA classification system.

Commodity Rates

Most CL and TL shipments move under commodity or exception rates. (Materials shipped under commodity rates are always in CL or TL lots.) A *commodity rate* is "a published tariff applicable to the shipment of a specific commodity in large quantities between selected geographical points" (NIGP Dictionary, 2021). Examples include coal, wheat, and gravel, which are commonly moved by ship, rail, or truck. Commodity rates are generally less expensive than class rates; but as recently as 2021, rates rose as companies worked to replenish stockpiles depleted during the Covid-19 pandemic (Anonymous, 2021). Rates are quoted on a per mile basis and usually include *deadhead miles* (i.e., miles traveled without cargo). A separate charge may be incurred for fuel surcharges, dependent on current market conditions, and can fluctuate.

Exception Rates

Carriers will publish exception rates that allow for different transportation characteristics for a commodity based on significant competition from other carriers or larger volume movements within a geographical area. An exception rate supersedes any previously published classification rate. However, there are other special rates designed to meet particular situations, which are briefly described below.

Freight All Kinds

Also known as all-commodity rates, carriers quote a rate in dollars per hundredweight or total dollars per shipment. Shipments are generally a mixed assortment of various types of freight going to one destination, and the cost to ship is the primary consideration rather than the freight's value.

Value Rates

Value rates are generally applicable in the movement of household goods. The liability to the carrier, based on the value of the freight, is the basis for the rate charged. A fixed amount of liability is determined, usually set at cents per pound.

Deferred Rates

Carriers may offer lower rates if the shipper is willing to accept a later arrival time. This rate allows the carrier greater flexibility in loading and moving the freight. UPS, FedEx, and the U.S. Postal Service are examples of organizations offering deferred rates.

Multiple-Vehicle Rates

Railroads may offer discounts to purchase transportation for multiple carloads of a particular commodity by offering multiple-vehicle rates. Lower transportation costs improve the railroads' economies of scale and make them more competitive with motor carriers. The *unit train rate* is an extension of multiple-vehicle rates, in which a rate is quoted for an entire train carrying one commodity.

Incentive Rates

A carrier may offer published incentive rates to encourage shippers to move larger loads, resulting in better utilization of equipment. The shipper pays a flat rate for freight up to a certain weight and then a lower rate for any freight above that weight.

Negotiated Rates

Carriers are frequently willing to negotiate rates. Consider the case of a shipper moving truckloads of freight on a regular basis; it could negotiate a lower rate. Additionally, discounts may be negotiated on LTL rates.

Joint Rates

A joint rate is used for hauling a single shipment over two or more independent transportation lines, which cooperate to offer a "through service." The shipment travels on one bill of lading.

Tapered Rates

Carriers' rates may increase but not directly proportional to the increase in distance. Tapered rates result when carriers can spread their fixed shipment costs over a greater number of miles traveled. A trucking firm may charge a rate of $ 43 to move freight 100 miles and $65 to move that same freight 200 miles. While the distance increased by 100%, the total cost was only about 34% more.

Stated Rates

A stated rate may be established for direct routes from one point to another. Rates via other routes between the same points are set in relation to the standard rate.

Through Rates

Through rates are applicable for transportation from point of origin to destination, including any stops in transit. However, a stop-off charge will be assessed for any intermediate stops. A through rate may be either a joint rate or a combination of two or more rates.

Differential Rates

A differential rate is the amount added to or subtracted from a through rate to establish a rate. For example, the rate from Chicago to Philadelphia is made up of the basis rate (Chicago to New York) less the differential basis (or rate) to Philadelphia.

Ocean Freight Rates

Ocean freight rates are typically quoted based on *weight ton* or *measurement ton*. A weight ton varies and is classified as:

- *short*, equal to 2,000 pounds;
- *long*, equal to 2,240 pounds; or
- *metric*, equal to 2,205 pounds.

A measurement ton is equal to 40 cubic feet. Carriers may also quote based on container rates. In addition, charges may be added to the cost of the shipment, which could include terminal handling fees, fuel adjustment factors, and adjustments for current rates.

Other Transportation Charges

Charges for services other than basic transportation may be incurred and will appear in the contract for service. Some of the possible charges are:

- limited access fee;
- bill of lading correction fee;
- advanced notification of delivery;
- driver assisted labor to load/unload freight;
- storage;
- hazardous materials surcharge;
- out-of-route miles;
- set-up/teardown;
- yard pulls; and
- use of lift gate.

Other fees are also charged as penalties, including:

- demurrage;
- detention;
- missing/late documentation; and
- overloads.

Terminal Services

Carriers own terminals where a number of functions may be performed, which will affect the transit time. For example, *dunnage*—material used to protect or support freight in or on rail cars and trucks—may be required. Bracing, false floors, and racks are common forms of dunnage. A specified amount of dunnage often can be used to transport a shipment without charging for the dunnage, but it is important to check the appropriate published tariff.

Smaller LTL shipments may be *consolidated* or *concentrated* at the terminal into one or more large shipments, to keep costs down. Shipments also arrive at the terminal for *dispersion*— the breaking down of a consolidated shipment into smaller shipments for individual consignees.

The carrier is obligated to load and unload LTL and LCL shipments. TL and CL shipments must be loaded by the shipper, but the consignee must unload; although the carrier is often willing to perform this function at an additional cost. Typically, a carrier will designate a certain amount of time for loading and unloading the vehicle. However, charges are assessed for vehicles detained beyond that point. *Demurrage* is the term used for storage charges assessed by railroads for rail cars, while *detention* applies to excessive storage of trucks or containers.

Consolidation and *dispersion* involve other *shipment service* functions, including billing, routing, and other clerical duties. The carrier must also maintain an adequate number of vehicles to meet shipping demands. Freight may be transferred at the terminal from one vehicle to another to provide through service.

Carriers also monitor shipments to assure they have been properly weighed and reach their intended destination. Carriers maintain proper weighing equipment and may be asked to reweigh a shipment should the shipper feel the original weight recorded was incorrect. Tracing is another common practice in the industry to determine the exact location of a shipment at any time during transit. Today, carriers offer shippers instant tracing through their websites. A carrier may be required to expedite a shipment by tracing it and then finding a way to decrease transit time. Shipments are sometimes miscarried or unloaded at the wrong terminal, which is called *free astray*. Free astray shipments are billed and forwarded to the correct terminal free of charge to the shipper.

Line-Haul Services

Line-haul services include additional services for the shipper while goods are in transit. *Diversion* and *reconsignment* are terms used interchangeably to describe a change in the shipment's consignee, consignor, routing, or original destination. However, *diversion* specifically applies to those changes in destination or routing before arrival of the shipment at the original destination, while *reconsignment* refers to changes in consignee before or after arrival of the shipment at the original destination (NIGP Dictionary, 2021); (Britannica.com, 2021). Shippers of perishable products commonly use this service. Shippers also have an option known as *transit privilege*, which allows them to store a shipment while in transit or to make changes that physically alter the shipment. For example, a shipper might stop a lumber shipment for additional processing before it continues to its final destination.

Shippers may choose to stop a shipment during transit to allow for loading or partial unloading, known as *stopping in transit*. The shipper pays charges based on the highest shipment weight at any time during transit. *Stop-off charges* are assessed for each intermediate step. A shipper may want to *pool* several LCL or LTL shipments into CL and TL shipments bound for one destination and single CL and TL shipments bound for one destination and one consignee. Carriers typically make the delivery to a warehouse or independently owned *drayage company*, which then breaks down the shipment and makes deliveries to individual consignees. Carriers often assign *pool cars* (rail) or *pool trucks* for specific industries, commodities, or locations. The total cost for this service is less than if the shipment was not originally pooled because the shipper is charged CL or TL rates.

Total Logistics Costs Concepts

The previous discussion has strictly focused on the costs and pricing of transportation. The goal of most shippers, in fact, is to minimize charges by the carrier. However, the decision should involve not only the costs of transportation but also other logistics costs, such as inventory holding costs and packaging costs, with the desired result being "overall" lower logistics expenditures. Known as a *systems approach*, the importance of each logistical function is recognized, but the interdependence of the various functions is also acknowledged. Thus, we recognize that there will be cost tradeoffs. Some of these logistical functions include the following:

- customer service (internal and external);
- documentation flows;
- order management and processing;
- warehouse site selection;
- recycling and disposal;
- warehouse management;
- demand forecasting;
- inventory management;
- packaging;
- supply management; and
- transportation management.

To illustrate, imagine that a county in Arizona might be able to reduce its overall logistics costs by consolidating several warehouses into one. This consolidation may result in higher transportation costs, but the offset still results in overall lower logistics costs. Similarly, a county in Washington may determine that shipping an order by truck rather than rail will result in higher transportation costs, but inventory-carrying costs will be reduced significantly because less inventory is required to meet internal end user requirements.

To implement a total logistics cost approach, there are two means of analysis. One method is *short-run*, or *static analysis* (Langley et al., 2021). Using this method, data is reviewed and compared at one point in time. Cost information is developed for each alternative, and a system is selected based on overall lowest costs. An example scenario is set out below.

Example: Short-Run (Static Analysis)

The City of New Amsterdam currently purchases mulch for several parks. The supplier delivers 25,000 cubic yards of mulch by rail to the city's centralized warehouse, where the mulch is bagged and then delivered by truck to each park. The city is considering a second alternative. The supplier would ship the mulch directly to each park by truck. To keep costs down, the total amount of mulch needed would be shipped at one time but deliveries would be made to each park. The tradeoff in this instance would be somewhat higher transportation costs of trucking versus the additional storage at the centralized warehouse and labor costs to bag and deliver the mulch to each park. The non-cost factor that the city might consider is customer service. Will the mulch be delivered more quickly and at the right time with the proposed system?

The second method is *long-run* or *dynamic analysis*. Break-even analysis is used to determine which of two or more logistics systems results in lower overall costs at a given volume of shipments. Fixed and variable costs are taken into consideration to evaluate the total cost for each alternative. However, the downside with break-even analysis is usually attributed to difficulty assigning costs to the fixed and variable categories. An example of long-run analysis is set out below.

Example: Long-Run (Dynamic) Analysis

The City of New Amsterdam is also interested in determining which alternative will be less expensive in the future, given that the department will be building new parks in the next two years and demand for mulch will increase. Under the current method of operation (Alternative 1), the city has fixed costs of $7,000 and pays $0.052 per bag in variable costs to deliver the mulch. Under the proposed system (Alternative 2), the department would pay lower fixed costs ($6,700) but higher variable costs ($0.065 to deliver the mulch).

The city uses the collected data to calculate the ***breakeven point*** or tradeoff point. This is the volume at which the city is indifferent to whether it chooses the first or second alternative. The problem can be set up as follows:

Current Method	=	**Alternative 1**
Total cost	=	Fixed cost + variable cost/unit * number of units
	=	$7,000 + $0.052x
Proposed Method	=	**Alternative 2**
Total cost	=	$6,700 + $0.065x

Tradeoff Point
$7,000 + $.052x = $6,700 + $0.065x
$3,00 = $0.013x
x = 23,077 cubic yards

Thus, if the city orders 23,077 cubic yards of mulch, it is indifferent as to whether it uses the first or second alternative. Because the city's demand is less than 23,077 cubic yards, it will be more cost effective to switch to the proposed system (Alternative 2); if demand exceeds the breakeven point, the existing system (Alternative 1) will be less expensive. To prove this point, the total costs for each alternative can be computed for a demand of 15,000 cubic yards:

Alternative 1
Total cost = $7,000 + $0.052 (15,000) = $ 7,780

Alternative 2
Total cost = $6,700 + $0.065 (15,000) = $ 7,675

The breakeven point can also be shown in the form of a graph (see Figure 4.3).

Should demand for mulch increase in the future, the city should redetermine the current fixed and variable costs and evaluate its transportation options.

Figure 4.3 Graphical representation of cost

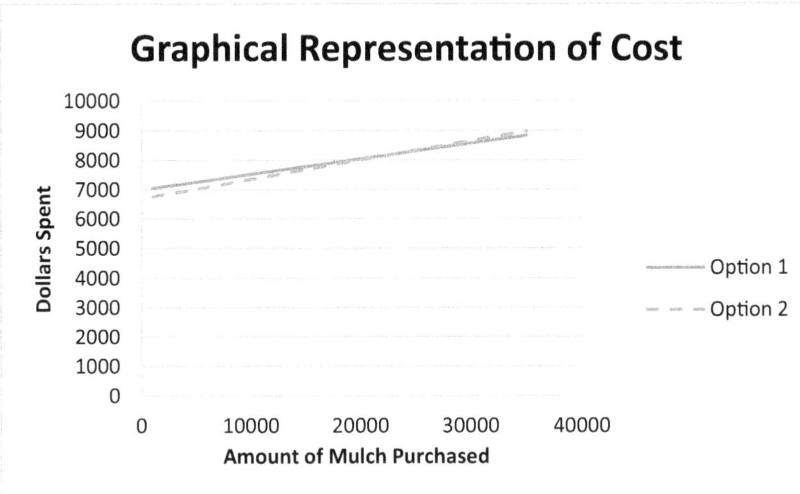

Conclusions

A number of factors can impact the rate that a shipper is charged for transporting materials. Whether it is based upon the type of goods being shipped, the distance they are traveling, or the number of containers used, a rate needs to be established so that all parties involved understand the cost of moving the materials from origin to destination. Professionals working within transportation and logistics should be familiar with the terminology of the shipping world in order to interact with shippers and third-party providers in the best way.

References

Anonymous (2021). "Commodity Shipping Rates Surge; Rally Isn't Over," Transport Topics, April 7. www.ttnews.com/articles/commodity-shipping-rates-surge-rally-isnt-over.

Bloomberg, D. J., LeMay, S., & Hanna, J. B. (2001). *Logistics.* Upper Saddle River, NJ: Prentice Hall.

Britannica.com (2021). "Diversion and reconsignment; stoppage in transit." www.britannica.com/topic/carriage-of-goods/Diversion-and-reconsignment-stoppage-in-transit.

Gilmore, Dan (2020). "The State of Logistics Union, 2020," Supply Chain Digest, June 25. www.scdigest.com/firstthoughts/20-06-25_State_of_Logistics_Report.php?cid=16943.

Grant, David B., Lambert, Douglas M., Stock, James R. and Lisa M. Ellram (2005). *Fundamentals of Logistics Management* (2nd ed.). New York: McGraw Hill.

Koenig, D (2021). "Southwest Airlines orders 100 Boeing 737 MAX Airplanes," AP News, March 29. https://apnews.com/article/business-04a4c13dea285869fabf6a36a0502231.

Langley, C. John, N., Robert A., Gibson, Brian J. and Coyle, J. J. (2021). *Supply Chain Management: A Logistics Perspective*. Boston, MA: Cengage Learning.

NIGP Dictionary (2021). www.nigp.org/dictionary-of-terms.

Novack, R., Gibson, B., Coyle, J. J. (2018). *Transportation: A Global Supply Chain Perspective* (9th ed.). Boston, MA: Cengage Learning.

Pfizer. "COVID-19 Vaccine U.S. Distribution Fact Sheet." www.pfizer.com/news/hot-topics/covid_19_vaccine_u_s_distribution_fact_sheet.

Rodriguez, J.-P. and Notteboom, T. (2020). "3.3 Transport Costs," *The Geography of Transport Systems*. New York: Routledge. https://transportgeography.org/contents/chapter3/transport-costs/.

Chapter 5

The Transportation Contract

Introduction

A sound contract can provide many advantages for an entity. Formal, written agreements that secure pricing, minimize risk, and protect an entity's interests are essential. These concepts also apply to transportation contracts. As for other buying agreements, the procurement professional is responsible for the transportation contract. From supplier sourcing through the solicitation process to contract award, and even to contract administration, the procurement professional ensures that everything comes together as planned. Transportation contracts should be viewed much like any other type of public contract. A report published by CAPS Research revealed that 67% of U.S. procurement departments are responsible for the management of transportation services (CAPS, 2011).

Negotiation and Transportation

Depending on the entity involved, the ability to negotiate may be limited. Many state and local entities can negotiate contracts, while others may have rules that prohibit negotiation on certain contract types. Historically, government entities have negotiated services for engineering, consulting, and information technology; but today, many entities are using the RFP process to

DOI: 10.4324/9781003298625-5

select other key service providers. According to NIGP: The Institute for Public Procurement, the RFP is a leading practice among U.S. public agencies, as it allows the procurement professional to apply judgment, experience, and professional knowledge (NIGP, 2019). Regardless of an individual entity's rules, there are concepts and strategies that will be useful in the contracting process.

Within this framework, all entities would seemingly perform some type of negotiation. Whether during the contract award process, amid a direct negotiation, haggling over change orders, or resolving contractor disputes, the procurement professional appears to be heavily involved in this arena. Negotiation is part of the day-to-day work environment in government. Work processes—including staffing resources, policy decisions, and budget appropriations—all require negotiation. Negotiation skills, therefore, become just as valuable internally as they are externally.

Carrier selection and the possible selection methods are decisions that need to be made. Transportation services can either be dealt with in a separate contract or be incorporated into the agreement for the goods purchased. The latter appears to be the most common approach in government. Whichever method is chosen, it is important that an entity address the transportation issue and ensure that a contract is in place to cover the service. As is the case with other contracts, specific contract terms that have been negotiated can prove invaluable, often "saving the day" for the entity.

Keys to Successful Negotiation

According to Johnson and Flynn (2020), the key to any successful negotiation is proper planning. This means that considerable thought and time should be devoted to the negotiation effort. Very likely, the other party will have spent time preparing for the negotiations so that its interests are protected. In a contract situation, the procurement professional must be very clear about the objectives of the entity. Is securing the lowest cost the main priority, or is it obtaining the highest level of service for the budgeted amount? Many of today's most successful negotiators prepare by developing a written negotiation plan. This document can include background information, key strategic issues, entity objectives, cost parameters, and entity concessions. A thorough plan can be very advantageous in assisting the procurement professional to prepare for negotiations and can help steer the focus toward key issues while keeping entity staff on track and the negotiation team on target.

Negotiation Plan

The following is an eight-step plan for carrying out negotiations. Each of these steps is important and, when executed together, should help ensure a successful negotiation. Figure 5.1 illustrates these steps.

Basic Groundwork

The first step is preparation, which includes understanding the facts of the situation, evaluating options and alternatives, and setting objectives. Suppliers

Figure 5.1 Negotiation steps

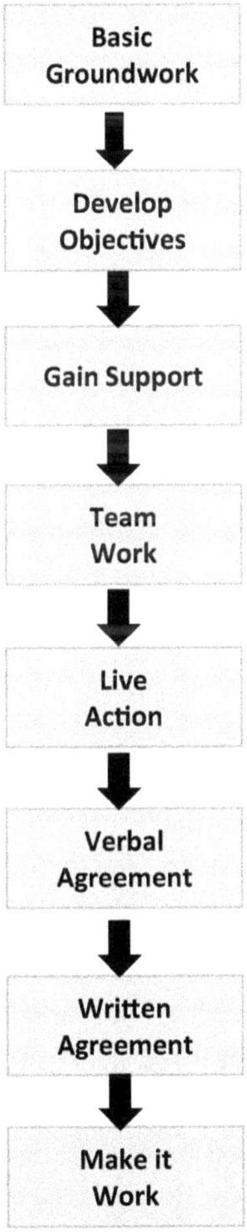

may provide useful information on past experiences with carriers. Carriers will also need to know about the entity, the products to be shipped, shipping destinations, special handling requirements, and service expectations. Some important tips to consider when going into a contract negotiation include the following (Robins, 2019):

- Do your due diligence on the supplier.
- Have a business conversation.
- Start fresh (especially with a new supplier).
- Address enforcement practicalities (venue, dispute resolution).
- Ensure services are properly defined.
- Require necessary insurance (e.g., cyber-liability).
- Include express performance requirements.

Objectives for the Negotiation Plan

To prepare a negotiation plan, specific objectives and strategies must be developed. This includes selecting the negotiation team, tactics, and site.

Gaining Support

Prior to the start of the negotiations, the negotiation team must have full management support and the negotiation plan must be consistent with entity objectives.

Teamwork

The team leader (i.e., lead negotiator) should convene a meeting with all members to discuss goals and strategies, and to review strengths and weaknesses. The role that each member will play, including the lead negotiator, should be well defined.

Live Action

This step includes the negotiation process itself, which should preferably take place face to face with the other party. Presentation, exploration, and hard bargaining are all part of the live action.

Verbal Agreement

Once both parties feel that they have reached agreement, the lead negotiator will ensure that key objectives have been met. Any uncertainties should be addressed before reaching verbal agreement.

Written Agreement

The written agreement will confirm and formalize the verbal agreement and will likely involve each party's legal counsel.

Making it Work

Complying with the terms of the agreement and making it work, for both parties, is the real test of its success. This is a good time to evaluate how well the negotiations went and to identify lessons learned for the next negotiation (Johnson & Flynn, 2020).

Tips on Negotiation

Some people are better negotiators than others. While it may seem that certain individuals are "naturals" when it comes to negotiating, they have likely invested time in training and practical application. Negotiation is identified by many organizations as a key attribute of world-class procurement and supply professionals. The Oxford College of Procurement and Supply notes that the ability to negotiate confidently is one of the most important skills a person can have. Also stressed is the need for preparation and active listening (Oxford, 2021).

Procurement professionals in the public sector need to develop their negotiation skills. The following are some general tips on what makes a good negotiator:

- Appreciate that both sides are under pressure, so there is no need to be intimidated.
- Want to learn new negotiating skills.
- Understand the art of negotiating.
- Be willing to practice.
- Want to create win/win situations.

Every negotiation is unique. There is a unique set of circumstances and issues surrounding each situation, which must be addressed by the parties involved. Some common principles can be applied to just about any situation involving negotiation. The following list presents some best practices in negotiation (NIGP, 2021):

- Create a detailed agenda for negotiation meetings.
- Let the other party speak to their objectives first.
- Ask questions and listen to understand what each party perceives as valuable.
- Observe the other party's body language.
- Use positive statements.
- Draw on the power of silence.
- Know and support your entity goals.

During the Covid-19 pandemic in 2020 and 2021, the need for virtual negotiation came to the forefront of supply chain management. With the ongoing need for entities to procure goods and services, supplier negotiations were often conducted via video conferencing platforms (e.g., Zoom, WebEx, Teams). Virtual negotiation is an important skill that stresses the importance of building a business relationship based upon trust and respect. Since nonverbal cues are tougher to notice in a virtual environment, it is important to regularly check on the state of the other party. Being clear in your communications and negotiation position will help keep the negotiation on track. Finally, silence in a virtual negotiation can be used to a party's advantage, much as it can be effective in an in-person negotiation (Fisher, 2020).

Scope of Negotiation

Within the public sector, there may not be a great deal of negotiation prior to the award of the contract. The crucial terms and conditions should be spelled out in the solicitation document, which usually becomes part of the resulting contract. Many entities include their standard form of contract within the solicitation documents so that all offerors can see what the resulting agreement will look like. There may be certain terms that can be negotiated, and these are the points that should be addressed prior to award. Whether the transportation is contracted for separately or as part of the goods procurement, the seasoned procurement professional will realize the importance of transportation specifics. The following figure notes the four elements of transportation costs. Managing these costs effectively is an important role for the procurement professional.

Figure 5.2 Elements of transportation costs

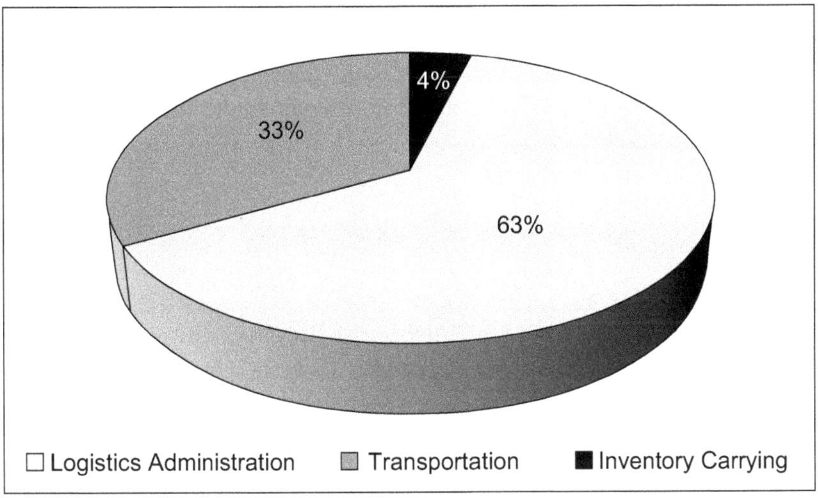

Adapted from: US Department of Transportation, Federal Highway Administration. Logistics Cost and US Gross Domestic Product. https://ops.fhwa.dot.gov/Freight/freight_analysis/econ_methods/lcdp_rep/index.htm

There are many key considerations when it comes to shipping. Entities need to consider these issues when developing solicitations and contracts, acknowledging that every issue is intended to protect the entity's interests and to minimize risk to the greatest extent possible.

Solicitation and Contract Award Considerations

Pricing Implications

A key aspect of any public contract is the pricing. The contract should include the pricing mechanisms used when the services are to be provided. How supplier billings are calculated, and whether they are set rates or discount percentages, should be addressed in written agreement. When negotiating with more than one carrier, it is important to use the same rate base consistently. Carriers publish individual rates, but they are often willing to negotiate based on competitors' rates or schedules published by regional rate bureaus. Once a common or "benchmark" rate is established, the procurement professional can then make a comparison based on discount levels.

Price may not be the most important element of the contract. If an RFP process used, service quality and capacity may be equally important. If the cost of transportation is included in the purchase of the goods, the contract should state that all costs and risks associated with the transportation of the goods are to be borne by the supplier. This is the effect of requiring the supplier's pricing to be FOB destination.

Price Changes

While pricing rates may be firm for an initial period, costs will likely escalate during the full life of the contract. In virtually all commodity areas, including transportation, prices are subject to change. When such instances do occur or are proposed by the contractor, there needs to be a common understanding of how this will be handled. It is unrealistic for procurement professionals to expect that the awarded prices will stay firm forever, but there does need to be a clear set of parameters within which prices can change. Perhaps the supplier can propose price increases on an annual basis (i.e., contract anniversary date), as long as the request is substantiated and documented. The rising costs of equipment, fuel, and labor are each likely to play a role. To limit the increase, such factors could be tied to a price index—either a local consumer price index, a PPI, or an industry-specific index. Increases should be formally changed in writing. This function is usually assigned to the procurement professional, who is familiar with the contract and can ensure that any price changes are properly evaluated and processed.

Performance Standards

Today's procurement professionals hold suppliers to a higher standard of performance. As the public sector moves away from transactional-based buying, the need for high-performing suppliers is more important than ever. According to the Chartered Institute of Procurement and Supply (CIPS) (2013), in order to determine world-class performance by a supplier, performance throughout the contract must be continuously monitored. Performance metrics must be agreed upon, including delivery times, allowable material defects, late shipments, material return parameters, and customer response time. These standards should be included in the contract so they can be accurately measured for compliance. The use of supplier scorecards has been successfully employed in the private sector for many years and is a practice that entities should consider. In addition to determining contract compliance, this can help a supplier improve its performance in areas like customer service, timely deliveries, and sustainable business practices.

If a contract calls for the outbound transport of materials, tangible timelines can be set for a response time for pickup requests and delivery time to the final destination—for instance, "carrier shall arrive at owner's dock within four hours of notification" and "contractor agrees to deliver materials shipped from the Salem, Oregon warehouse to the Ontario, Canada plant site within a 24-hour period." The use of "shall" denotes the imperative in contract clauses, while the use of "may" is permissive or optional (NIGP, 2004). It is important that procurement professionals are familiar with these terms and know how and when to use each appropriately. As with any contract, the important areas of performance must be noted in such a way that they can be monitored during the contract.

Packaging

The proper packaging of goods can protect them from weather and rough handling during transit and ensure they are in good condition when they reach the buyer's dock.

Many of the goods that are delivered to entities are in packaging provided by the manufacturer. Depending on the types of goods being shipped, they may be surrounded by foam peanuts in a cardboard box or strapped to a wooden pallet. Whatever the case, the procurement professional wants to be certain that the goods being purchased will be adequately protected while being transported. As an example, a microscope being purchased for a police forensic lab is worth thousands of dollars, while the material protecting it is worth just a few dollars. However, the protection may very well save the procurement professional time and money in filing for damages and waiting for a new shipment if the equipment is damaged.

For larger shipments, there are obviously different packaging requirements. Perhaps potting soil is being purchased for the parks department, and the contract specifies a certain size of bag. Multiple bags are stacked on a pallet, shrink wrapped, and then delivered by truckload to their destination. Even pallets have varied specification, including two-way versus four-way entry, composite material versus wood, and returnable versus non-returnable. So even with a purchase for something as basic as potting soil, the buyer must realize there are additional considerations related to transport.

The type of packaging that is required should correlate to the available warehouse storage space. If an end user does not have industrial shelving, it is unlikely that palletized bulk material will do it much good. In those cases, smaller containers and packaging should be specified. Consideration must be given to the cost of carrying large quantities of material, the cost of bulk material versus smaller shipments, and the packaging standards within a given industry. Suppliers may be willing to package goods in whatever way is requested; but if it is non-standard for them, the price will inevitably increase. One can see that something as seemingly simple as packaging can actually be quite complex.

Consideration should be given as to whether the packaging is recyclable. Governments are focusing on sustainability issues in procurement more than ever. The incorporation of sustainability into the procurement strategy and resulting contract is recognized as a best practice by leading organizations (NIGP, 2012). For a contract involving transportation, requirements can be put in place that reduce non-sustainable packaging and limit the material that ultimately ends up in landfill.

Reparations

There are occasions when a regulated carrier improperly charges the shipper for transportation aside from loss and damages. Incorrect charges may occur due to duplicate billing, overcharging, or improperly routing a shipment. When refund payments or rebates are made to the shipper to remedy this situation, they are referred to as *reparations*. The need to file for reparations is discovered during an audit of bills of lading. A complaint is then filed with the Surface Transportation Board, which determines the extent of reparations required (www.stb.gov/resources/need-assistance/rcpa/). Federal law (U.S. Code, Title 49—Transportation) requires carriers to repay, to the extent possible, all amounts due plus interest.

Overcharges and Undercharges

Overcharges and *undercharges* are just as their names imply. Based on the correct shipping rate, the amount paid to the carrier is either more or less than is owed. On the government side, the procurement professional is responsible for not overpaying the entity's freight bills. An overpayment can occur when the entity does not pay the freight bill in a timely manner. If the carrier sends a second invoice, the possibility of a double payment for the same shipment of goods may exist.

Most carriers are careful to ensure that they are not undercharging their customers. While the carrier certainly wants to collect the full dollar amount owed, it is also legally bound not to undercharge. To charge some customers less than others would constitute discriminatory pricing, which is illegal.

Conducting a freight bill audit can determine whether overcharges or undercharges exist, but can also be an added expense to the entity. Such an audit can be handled internally or externally. An internal audit is conducted by the entity's own employees, who review freight bills and purchase files for discrepancies. If an outside independent company is used, this is referred to as an external audit. A common arrangement is an agreement that the independent company will keep a set percentage of any overcharges found. The entity awarding the contract will specify how such an audit should be conducted.

Loss and Damages

Despite each party's best efforts, there is always the possibility of loss or damage during shipment. *Loss* refers to goods purchased that are missing; as opposed to *damaged* goods, which actually arrive but are not in an acceptable condition. Normally, whichever party owns the goods during shipment is responsible for the loss or damage. That is a key reason to address the transfer of ownership in the contract or purchase order. The most common term for delivery is *FOB Destination Freight Prepaid and Allowed.*

The proper receipt of goods by the entity is important. According to Johnson and Flynn (2020), the receiving department generally checks incoming shipments to ensure that:

- the goods were actually ordered by the entity;
- no visible damage occurred during transit;
- the quantities received are correct; and
- the shipping documentation is complete.

The extent of the supplier's obligations should be covered in the agreement in the event of lost or damaged goods. Ideally, the contractor should assume the burden of tracing the lost shipment or replacing the damaged goods. The entity also may want to add a provision stating that the goods will be replaced within a certain period of time and reserve the right to replace the goods through other means at the contractor's expense.

Expediting and Tracing

Expediting occurs if the buyer wishes to accelerate the agreed-upon delivery time. Expediting differs from routine follow-up or checking to determine if the order will be received as expected. Depending on the goods that are en route, the shipment may be highly critical. For example, a repair part is being shipped for the water department and is now needed sooner than originally anticipated. The procurement staff or supplier makes arrangements with the carrier, either before shipment or at some stopping point, to adjust the delivery time.

Tracing occurs when the buyer wishes to follow the shipment during transport. Goods may be transported via multiple modes, which requires a detailed understanding of how the various carriers handle their freight. Most often, the procurement professional can request the bill of lading, which will contain a unique number allowing the shipment to be traced. There should be a provision in the contract on how shipment tracing will be provided.The entity should have a supplier contact person to perform this function and provide the shipping status within an agreed timeframe. A common turnaround time for this information is within 24 hours. When the supplier's representative attempts to trace a shipment, they need the following, at a minimum:

- the bill of lading;
- a description of material; and
- the date shipped.

Considered the most important transportation document, the bill of lading is a hauler or carrier's contract, which may also act as the receipt of goods transported and delivered to the consignee (NIGP, 2010). The bill of lading is normally prepared by the shipper's logistics or traffic department but is legally issued by the carrier. U.S. government bills of lading are used when government supplies, materials, or personal property is transferred. Commercial carriers use their own forms, but they are standardized by industry and are generally negotiable. A negotiable or "order" bill of lading allows title or ownership of a shipment to be endorsed over to another party other than the original receiver. If a non- negotiable or "straight" bill of lading is issued, however, goods are consigned directly to the receiver and are generally delivered by the carrier without surrender of the bill of lading.

Force Majeure

Force majeure is a French term that refers to conditions that may occur that are outside of the control of either party. Circumstances that might prevent the supplier from performing in accordance with the contract include floods, earthquakes, tornadoes, and even war. Because the supplier has neither fault nor control in such instances, the buyer cannot penalize the supplier for nonperformance. If a critical shipment was a week late due to a snowstorm during which no normal transportation could get through, the entity would need to make whatever arrangements it could to address the material shortage. They would do so at their own cost because the supplier cannot be held liable. If a *force majeure* clause is not included in the contract, a legal action still may result on the basis that the clause should be implied under the doctrine of commercial frustration (Hinkelman, 2010).

Contract Term

The length of time an agreement is in place is referred to as the *contract term*. This is established upfront in the contract process and should be carefully considered. Generally, a longer-term contract will secure the most competitive rates, as transportation providers find such guaranteed business very attractive. For example, if a supplier knows it has an entity's business for three years with an option for two more, it will do all it can to submit a very favorable offer. A short-term contract (e.g., one year) will likely mean higher pricing and fewer concessions.

It is a good idea to consider renewals or extensions to the original contract term. Often an entity will make an initial one-year contract award and then consider renewals on an annual basis. This is a sound strategy, as it provides an incentive for the supplier to perform well during the initial term. Knowing that additional business is on the line will help keep the origination's deliveries a priority and on time.

Case Study: Strategic Partnership in the Rose City

After years of contracting with trucking providers to transport waste at the lowest possible cost, Metro, the regional government of Portland, Oregon, embarked on an RFP to establish a strategic partnership. Its solicitation process included public meetings seeking input from community members and transportation providers. Ultimately, an RFP was issued that encouraged innovation and sustainable business practices. While cost was a factor in Metro's selection process, other factors that drove its decision were sustainable business practices, cleaner burning truck engines, and economic sustainability. The agency selected Walsh Trucking, of Troutdale, Oregon, to provide hauling services in the region for a period of 10 years. This long-term partnership brought a valued service to the Portland area, complied with its regulatory waste requirements, and provided dozens of family wage jobs.

Demurrage and Detention

When a buyer keeps a railcar longer than the parties have agreed upon, the carrier can assess a demurrage charge. *Demurrage* is like rent and is a monetary amount that the buyer is obligated to pay for such retention. Imagine that an organization purchases a carload of fertilizer. The carrier drops the delivery at the entity's warehouse with the understanding that the entity will have two days to unload it. After that time, the rail car will be scheduled for pickup so that the carrier can transport other shipments. If the entity experiences a delay in unloading the goods and keeps the trailer a third day, the carrier will bill for demurrage. This will be an additional charge and will increase the cost of the original delivery.

Detention refers to the holding of a motor carrier's driver, truck, trailer, or railroad container beyond a specified timeframe. Excessive holding may result in detention charges being assessed to the consignor or consignee. The *consignor* is the party that ships the goods, while the *consignee* is the person or company (usually the buyer) to which the goods are to be delivered.

During international shipments, delays in clearing goods through Customs can also result in detention charges. In this situation, demurrage applies to the cargo, while detention generally applies to the equipment (Hinkelman, 2010).

Because demurrage and detention are issues that will have a financial impact on the buyer, they need to be clearly spelled out in the agreement. What are the grace periods, if any, for the entity; and what charges will be assessed if those periods are surpassed? Having these terms agreed upon can avoid much discussion and debate at a later time.

Conflicts and Disputes

Despite everyone's best efforts and intentions, inevitably, disputes arise during contract performance. It could be a disagreement over a delivery schedule, a difference over a freight bill, or countless other issues. The goal of each party should be to resolve the conflict in some mutually acceptable manner. When conflicts within the supply chain arise, they can be resolved basically in three ways:

- litigation;
- acceptance; or
- negotiation.

(Hutchins, 2002)

Normally, litigation is the least preferred option, as it relies on attorneys and judges to settle the differences. It is an expensive and usually time-consuming process. Additionally, it often results in ill will between the parties for years to come. Some disputes will inevitably wind up in the courts. Recognition and acceptance of the issue is another approach. However, unwillingness to accept that a conflict exists can lead to larger long-term issues. The ideal approach is to negotiate the differences between the parties. By using accomplished negotiation skills, the procurement professional can reach a settlement that is acceptable to both parties without litigation. A resolution that leaves both parties feeling content is referred to as a "win-win."

The standard contract used by an entity may specify arbitration or mediation as a possible method to settle any disputes. Procurement professionals should be aware of these formal contract requirements and should participate in establishing these requirements. They should also attempt to resolve differences at the operational level so that contract performance can continue for the entity.

Package Delivery Services

While contracting for large or complex shipments via motor carriage or rail freight is important, the need for package delivery services should not be overlooked in the public sector. Particularly for small entities, the use of carriers like UPS and FedEx for small package delivery may comprise the largest portion of their shipping expenditure. A local fire authority, for instance, may need small parts delivered daily, so focusing on package delivery services will be beneficial.

Cost and service are prime issues of consideration when contracting for package delivery. The corporate rates for national delivery companies are quite competitive, but it may be advantageous for small entities to employ a separate contract for these services. This is an ideal opportunity to utilize a cooperative contract awarded by a larger entity. Many state procurement departments issue requirements contracts for such services that are available to governmental entities throughout the area. In these cases, set rates are negotiated and must be monitored. Routine monitoring by the procurement professional can help provide valuable cost control for the entity.

The entity should be familiar with the terms of the contract so that the service aspect can be monitored. Service factors such as delivery time, shipment tracking, and package "will calls" should be addressed. Knowing the services required of the shipping company, and holding it responsible for those requirements, is the key for small and large entities. In addition to national firms like UPS and FedEx, there are also many local companies that provide package deliveries. These smaller local companies can have a niche in public contracting, as they can offer a viable option for procurement professionals. Like other service and commodity areas, the competitive environment within this industry can help ensure favorable pricing and services. Package delivery providers will continue to play a valuable role for government in meeting freight transportation needs.

Conclusions

The transportation contract is an important instrument in public procurement. It includes terms and conditions that protect an entity's interests during the shipment of its goods. Regardless of which solicitation method is used, the resulting contract should be thorough and sound, and include certain provisions. Pricing and price changes are important, but so are contract terms and renewals. When something does go wrong during transit, issues such as shipment tracing, damages, and disputes can all come to the forefront. While each contract situation is unique, many issues remain consistent whether the contract is for motor, rail, or air transport. Agreements with freight forwarders, brokers, or 3PLs need careful attention. In addition to performing their own research and using their own expertise, procurement professionals should consider the use of transportation consultants to assist in the negotiation process (Gentry, 1991). The ability to negotiate is a key skill in the public sector. Whether it is utilized during supplier selection or after contract award, it can be a valuable tool. Certain techniques can be employed to help ensure a favorable result for the procurement professional's entity. Being prepared at the onset of negotiations—even just developing a negotiation plan—can mean the difference between success and failure. Laying the internal groundwork and developing objectives and desired outcomes can help all entity representatives operate as a team. Once a verbal agreement is reached between the parties, a written agreement should be drafted by the entity.

Today's procurement professionals need to be well versed in contracting for services and able to negotiate when needed. This can help ensure that the entity's goods arrive in the right condition, at the right price, and at the right time. As logistics services such as transportation continue to be outsourced by the government, the need to develop strong, detailed contracts will continue to be a requirement of the procurement professional.

References

Center for Advanced Procurement Strategies Research (2012). *Supply's Organizational Roles and Responsibilities.* Institute for Supply Management: Tempe, AZ.

Chartered Institute of Procurement & Supply (2013). *Monitoring the Performance of Suppliers*. London, UK: CIPS Knowledge.
Dawson, R. (1999). *The Secrets of Power Negotiation* (2nd edn.). Franklin Lakes, NJ: Career Press.
Duffy, R. J. (1999). "Logistics: A custom link," Purchasing Today, 10(3), March.
Fisher, P. (2020). "Eight Things to Know About the Art of Virtual Negotiation," University of Oxford, Said Business School. www.sbs.ox.ac.uk/oxford-answers/eight-things-know-about-art-virtual-negotiation.
Flynn, M., Buffington, K., and Pennington, R. (2020). *Legal Aspects of Public Procurement*. London, UK: Routledge.
Gentry, J. J. (1991). *Purchasing's Involvement in Transportation Decision Making*. Tempe, AZ: Center for Ad vanced Purchasing Studies.
Hinkelman, E. G. (2010). *Dictionary of International Trade*. Novato, CA: World Trade Press.
Hutchins, G. (2002). *Supply Management Strategies for Improved Performance*. Portland, OR: Working It, LLC.
Johnson, F. & Flynn, A. (2020). *Purchasing and Supply Management* (16th edn.). New York: McGraw-Hill.
Konezny G. P., & Beskow, M. J. (1999). *Third Party Logistics: Improving Global Supply Chain Performance*. Minneapolis, MN: Piper Jaffray Equity Research.
Leenders, M. R., & Flynn, A. E. (1995). *Value Driven Purchasing*. New York: AMACOM, American Management Association.
National Association of State Procurement Officials (NASPO). (2001). *Survey of State and Local Government Purchasing Principles and Practices*. Lexington, KY: NASPO.
National Institute of Governmental Purchasing, Inc. (NIGP). (2021). *Public Procurement Practice, Negotiation*. Herndon, VA: NIGP.
National Institute of Governmental Purchasing, Inc. (NIGP) (2012). *Public Procurement Practice, Sustainable Procurement Practices*. Herndon, VA: NIGP.
National Institute of Governmental Purchasing, Inc. (NIGP) (2019). *Public Procurement Practice, Request for Proposal*. Herndon, VA: NIGP.
National Institute of Governmental Purchasing, Inc. (NIGP) (2010). *Public Procurement Dictionary of Terms*. Herndon, VA: NIGP.
National Institute of Governmental Purchasing, Inc. (NIGP) (2004). *The Legal Aspects of Public Purchasing*. Herndon, VA: NIGP.
Oxford College of Procurement & Supply (2021). "Top Seven Skills for Procurement Negotiations." www.oxfordcollegeofprocurementandsupply.com/top-seven-skills-for-successful-procurement-negotiations/.
Robins, M. (2019). "Getting Your Deal: 12 Tips for Shippers Negotiating Freight Contracts," Material Handling & Logistics, July 29. www.mhlnews.com/transportation-distribution/article/22055714/getting-your-deal-12-tips-for-shippers-negotiating-freight-contracts.
Schubert, H. (2019). "Get Basic Tips for Negotiating Freight Contracts," The Balance Small Business, November 20. www.thebalancesmb.com.
Stroh, M. B. (2006). *A Practical Guide to Transportation and Logistics (3rd edition)*. Dumont, NJ: Logistics Network, Inc.

Chapter 6

Global Transportation

Introduction

Global trade is a fact of life. Manufacturers can produce goods around the world and rely on fast transportation to move those goods from one country to another. A trend of rising imports confirms this. Over the past 20 years, imports of goods and services have almost doubled, increasing from $1.45 trillion in 2000 to $2.81 trillion in 2020 (U.S. Census Bureau, 2021). In many instances, government procurement tends to favor local suppliers because of tradition and simplicity. However, increasing competition from foreign suppliers can put pressure on domestic suppliers to reduce costs. The end result can be more value for the taxpayer's dollar. Foreign goods can also be of higher quality, resulting in better service levels. If an entity is considering buying from foreign suppliers, there should be a clear understanding of the issues involving logistics and transportation.

Because the distance goods travel from the supplier to the buying entity is longer, there are factors to consider such as inventory decisions of when and how much to buy. While the choice of modes of transportation is the same as when buying domestically, a combination of modes most likely will be needed. Also, certain carriers and third parties specialize in international shipments to the United States and can help smooth the process. The legal environment also must be considered. While many nations have deregulated their own transportation systems, regulations between countries remain strict in most instances. Lastly, agreements between countries also may be negotiated through bilateral or multilateral agreements, but additional paperwork will be involved. Given

DOI: 10.4324/9781003298625-6

these complexities, this chapter takes a deeper look into the issues related to the logistics of global transportation.

Why Buy Global?

There are many reasons for buying from global suppliers, but most procurement professionals do so because they feel they are getting more value for the dollar. Johnson (2019) lists 10 reasons to purchase from a foreign supplier; six of these specifically apply to government procurement.

Advantages

Lower Overall Cost of Ownership

The cost of ownership may be lower because of lower labor costs, better exchange rates, and more efficient equipment and processes. Suppliers also may focus production on specific products to gain economies of scale. Tariffs in many instances have been reduced, keeping the overall cost—including logistics-related costs—down.

Quality

Quality, although not necessarily better, may be more consistent because foreign suppliers own newer and better equipment, with better quality control systems in place and an emphasis on zero defects (producing products right the first time).

Availability

Items may not be widely available domestically, including raw materials such as rare earth metals found mostly in China and manufactured goods such as computer printers or cellphones.

Efficiencies

Foreign suppliers may provide faster delivery than domestic suppliers, or ship and hold inventory locally until the product is needed by the customer. Global trade management software (GTM) can be used by procurement professionals to collaborate with global trade partners, and streamline trade and manage operations more effectively and efficiently. For example, specialty chemicals company Altana uses GTM to track shipments with export limits to avoid delays (Kroll, 2020). Better technical services may be offered if the international supplier has a good distribution network in place. These services can include a better assortment of parts fitted to the customer's needs, technical advice, and customer service.

Technological superiority

Advanced technologies may be offered by global suppliers, especially in primary metals such as steel. For example, TSMC, based in Taiwan, and Samsung Electronics, based in South Korea, dominated in 2021 with over 70% of the semiconductor market (Kharpal, 2021).

Challenges

While there are advantages, global suppliers should be vetted for reliability and responsiveness, similar to domestic suppliers. An entity additionally needs to recognize that it may lack sufficient resources to manage its local suppliers and also qualify new global suppliers. When the dollar value of the contract is high, site visits are important, even though they may be expensive and time consuming. Other challenges identified in selecting global sources include the following.

Language Barriers

While English is the international language of business, there still are many who are not fluent, and interpreters may be required.

Time Differences

Although it may be daytime in the United States, other countries operate in different or even opposite time zones. For example, the United States and China are 12 hours apart. Some accommodation will need to be made when verbal and other forms of communication such as email and text are necessary.

Quality Expectations

There can be no assumptions when it comes to quality. Quality specifications should be put in writing and confirmed with the carrier.

Environmental and Labor Compliance Issues

Many developing countries (e.g, India and other Asian countries) have lower environmental standards than those specified by the World Health Organization, and do not have the capability to monitor and enforce the existing regulations (Zhao, 2019). Another issue is labor. More than half of all employees in developing countries do not receive the benefits to which they are entitled. This could be because the enforcement of labor laws has been politicized; or because either there is a lack of inspectors to enforce the laws or the inspectors are corrupt (Ronconi, 2019).

Longer Lead Times

Shipping by water naturally takes longer. There is also the issue of time in port to sort, unload, and reload goods or containers for shipment domestically. In 2021, there was a shortage of containers due to increased consumer demand for goods, creating delays in deliveries as ports such as Los Angeles and Long Beach were overwhelmed (Miller, 2021).

Higher Shipping Costs

Because more than one mode of transportation is typically required, shipping charges can add up. Also, as demand increases, so do shipping rates. In 2021, demand for goods soared and along with it, shipping rates. For example, freight rates from China to the United States increased over 150% from 2020 to 2021 due to strong consumer demand (Brett, 2021). Good brokers keep abreast of these changes and can be helpful in finding the most cost-effective combination of carriers.

Poor Logistics Infrastructure

Not all suppliers have the reliable and predictable logistics systems found in the United States, particularly in less sophisticated countries. For example, while Mexico is the United States' top trading partner (see Figure 6.1), it ranks

Figure 6.1 U.S. top trading partners in goods, 2022 ($ billions)

Rank	*Country*	*Total trade*	*Percentage*
1	Mexico	262.8	14.77
2	Canada	258.3	14.5
3	China	248.7	13.9
4	Japan	86.0	4.8
5	Germany	80.1	4.5
6	South Korea	64.2	3.6
7	United Kingdom	47.4	2.7
8	Vietnam	44.6	2.5
9	India	43.1	2.4
10	Taiwan	42.9	2.4

Source: United States Census Bureau (2022). "Top Trading Partners – January 2022." census.gov/foreign-trade/statistics/highlights/toppartners.html.

53 out of 167 countries for its logistics performance. As stated by the World Bank:

> Trade has become a 24/7 business and good performance in trade requires connectivity along not only roads, rail, and sea, but in telecommunications, financial markets, and information-processing. Having inefficient or inadequate systems of transportation, logistics, and trade-related infrastructure can severely impede a country's ability to compete on a global scale.
>
> (Anonymous, 2021)

For the procurement professional, longer lead times may be needed to account for poor infrastructure.

Currency Exchange Risks

The primary risk is known as *transaction risk*, which results in fluctuations from the time of payment for a product/service to the actual settlement date. This risk can be mitigated in several ways. One of the most common is the use of forward contracts, which fixes the exchange rate in advance. Another option is the stop loss order, which allows procurement to set a minimum acceptable exchange rate to carry out the transfer.

Political Instability

Less developed countries are more susceptible to political unrest. For example, in July 2021, there were protests and violence in South Africa because the country's former president was arrested. This "forced shipping lines to shut depots, warehouses and cold stores in Durban and Johannesburg," leading to shipping delays (Wackett, 2021; Supply Chain Quarterly Staff, 2015).

Current Trends

There are several trends occurring in the global marketplace that specifically relate to logistics. First, there has been overall growth in world trade. As shown in Figure 6.2, both exports and imports have continued upward, with a couple of exceptions. As recently as 2020, imports and exports were down due to the global pandemic, but they rebounded in 2021 (UNCTAD, 2021). Logistics has made this possible through better planning and information technology, improved trade agreements among nations, and faster means of transportation.

A second trend is the growth of containers used in international trade. Containers are moved on some form of cargo vessel, carrying primarily semi-manufactured and manufactured products. From 2000 to 2017, the tonnage carried in containers increased from 102 metric tons to 1.83 billion metric tons (Statista, 2021). In 2021, no single container ship company dominated the market.

Container ship operators often use vessel-sharing agreements to improve service. In essence, they agree to operate service along a specific trade route

Figure 6.2 International trade in goods and services

Year	*Balance of Trade*	*Exports*	*Imports*
2000	−369,685	1,082,963	1,452,648
2005	−716,543	1,291,503	2,008,046
2010	−503,090	1,872,318	2,375,408
2012	−525,906	2,247.453	2,773,359
2014	−483,952	2,392,615	2,876,566
2016	−475,474	2,244,337	2,719,811
2018	−580,950	2,538,638	3,119,588
2020	−676,684	2,134,441	2,811,125

Source: United States Census Bureau. census.gov/foreign-trade/statistics/historical/index.html/.

Figure 6.3 Shipping alliances, 2019

Alliance	*Vessels*	*Total capacity (million TEUs)*	*Market*
2M: Maersk and MSC	185	2.1	Europe, Asia, United States
Ocean: COSCO, OOCL, CMA, CGM, Evergreen	330	3.8	Asia-Europe, Asia-Middle East
The Alliance: Hapag-Lloyd, ONE, Yang Ming, HMM	249	4.019	Asia, North America, Central America, South America, Mediterranean, Indian Subcontinent, Middle East

Source: Frese, F. (2019). Shipping Alliances: 2M, Ocean Alliance and THE Alliance. https://container-xchange.com/blog/shipping-alliances/.

using a specified number of vessels. The amount of space allocated to each partner can vary from port to port depending on the agreement made (Anonymous, 2021). The purpose of these agreements is to expand service and reduce costs. Another way to expand service is through slot charter agreements. One shipping line contracts with another for "slots" or container space on a ship. One slot holds one 20-foot container. These agreements are made within shipping alliances. Alliances share information such as stowage plans, scheduling, and vessel assignments. As shown in Figure 6.3, there were three major shipping alliances in 2019, with a combined capacity of almost 10 million 20-foot equivalent units (TEUs) (i.e., the number of 20-foot containers [Frese, 2019]).

A third trend is the adoption of new technologies, similar to other industries. For example, shipping lines have begun to digitize the supply chain and buy into shipping platforms supported by blockchain technology. Tradelens, a "neutral industry platform," connects a network of supply chain partners— including shippers, carriers, third parties, ports, and customs— which increases transparency and secure data transmission. In 2021, more than 300 entities were connected through Tradelens and this number is expected to grow (Tradelens, 2021).

A fourth trend is the increase in trade agreements. Preferential trade agreements give advantages such as zero or lower tariffs to certain trading partners. These agreements have continued to climb. According to the World Bank, there were more than 330 such recorded agreements worldwide in 2021 (World Bank, 2021). The advantages of these agreements include reduced red tape, less documentation, and freer movement of traffic at national borders.

In 2020, the North American Trade Agreement was replaced with the United States-Mexico-Canada Trade Agreement. Besides preferential treatment, this new agreement seeks to update and rebalance reciprocal trade, and addresses current issues such as digital trade and anticorruption (Office of the United States Trade Representative, 2020). In 2019, the Mercosur trading bloc (Argentina, Brazil, Paraguay, and Uruguay) reached an agreement with the European Union— subject to legal review and final approval of the member nations—to increase bilateral trade and economic integration (Hartman, 2021).

The World Trade Organization (WTO) has been a catalyst for improved trade relations. Comprised of 164 nation members, the WTO is the only international organization dealing with rules of trade between countries (World Trade Organization, 2021). It functions to provide a forum for trade negotiations, handle trade disputes, monitor national trade policies, and provide technical and trade assistance to developing nations. The WTO's guiding principles are that the trading system should:

- function without discrimination between trading partners;
- be freer, with barriers coming down through negotiation;
- be predictable, without arbitrary tariffs or other non-tariff barriers;
- be more competitive, eliminating export subsidies, product dumping, and similar practices; and
- be more beneficial to less developed countries.

International Transportation Choices

Ocean Transportation

Ocean transportation is the most important and most common form of transportation for international shipments. As shown in Figure 6.4, maritime trade increased during the 2000s, growing about 3% annually from 2010 to 2018.

Ocean vessels are typically used to move lower-valued products with a high density. Sea freight is generally categorized by type, including:

- main bulks—coal, grains, ores, fertilizers, alumina, bauxite, sugar;
- tankers—petroleum, chemicals, fertilizers;
- containerized non-bulk items; and
- other dry cargo.

There are several forms of service offered, with distinctive differences. *Liners*, often called *freighters*, carry mostly general cargo and offer space to any shipper. They offer regularly published schedules with specific routes, sailing whether they are full or not. They charge set tariffs or rates depending on the cargo type,

Figure 6.4 Maritime trade

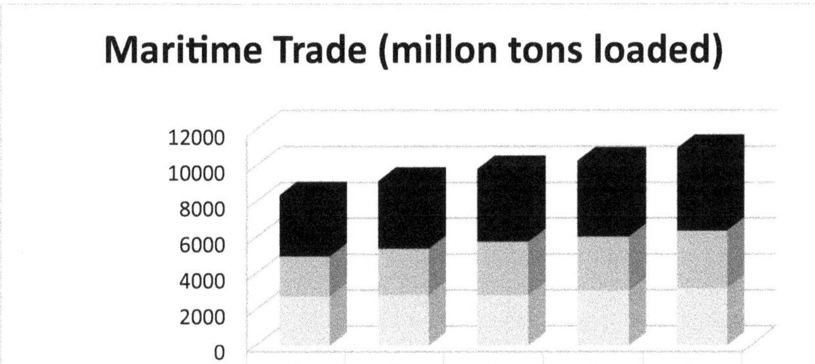

	1	2	3	4	5
Other Dry Cargo	3423	3791	4054	4228	4601
Main Bulks	2232	2564	2964	3009	3210
Tankers	2752	2840	2825	3058	3194

Source: INCTAD, https://hbs.unctad.org/world-seaborne-trade/.

weight, and distance shipped. Tariffs may be published on their website or through an independent party. A large volume of their tonnage is dedicated to container ships or a combination of containers and other cargo. Large steamship companies generally own liners, with a few belonging to *shipping conferences*, also known as *liner conferences*.

Shipping conferences, formed around 1870, are associations of shipping lines offering service for a given sea route on conditions agreed upon by the members (Branch, 1989). Considered semi-monopolistic in nature, they were originally established to create a bond between shippers and carriers: shippers would use only conference vessels, and conferences agreed to charge lower rates than if a shipper used a non-conference carrier. Conference members were also allowed to *pool* or share vessels to eliminate competition and reduce costs. If a conference member used a U.S. port, *service contracts* could be negotiated with shippers. With a service contract, the shipper agreed to ship a minimum volume of cargo—usually defined in TEUs. Set rates were based on an intermodal, point-to-point, or port-to-port basis. The carrier guaranteed regular service and specialized equipment over a set period.

The conference system has weakened since the United States passed the Ocean Shipping Reform Act of 1998 (OSRA) (Gourdin, 2001). As of May 1999, liner carriers can enter into confidential service contracts. However, carriers may not charge anything other than their published tariff rates or service contract rates. Groups of shippers can also enter into service contracts, although non-vessel-operating common carriers (NVOCCs) are prohibited from doing so. While carriers retain their antitrust immunity on agreements filed with the FMC, they are still required to meet the common carrier obligation of the Shipping Act of 1984. Tariff filing with the FMC was eliminated and replaced by electronic publication through private services or websites. During the first year of OSRA, more than 46,000 new service contracts were filed with the FMC—an increase of 124% over 1998 and a strong indicator of their popularity. Many carriers also left their conferences, setting their own rates and relying on vessel-sharing agreements. In 2008 the European Union forbade the use of liner conferences, further weakening the system. Most carriers that use liner conferences today are small to medium-sized entities.

A second form of carriage is the *charter ship*, where the vessel owners contract with a shipper/charterer for a specific voyage, known as *voyage charter*, or for a specific period of time, known as *time charter*. The charterer pays all operating costs during the contract period, and the vessel owner provides the crew. A charterer can carry any cargo other than that which is prohibited by the contract.

Bareboat charters, also known as *demise charters*, are a third option. Full control of the vessel is transferred to the charterer, which hires the crew, pays all operating expenses, and accepts full responsibility for the vessel. Ship brokers generally make arrangements for charters, keeping track of the location and status of ships. The shipper contacts the broker, which negotiates a price that includes a broker commission.

Finally, private ocean carriers owned by the shipper are another option. Private carriage is often used to lower costs or have more control.

International Airlines

Movement of air freight *vis-à-vis* air transportation has become increasingly popular with the advent of more frequently scheduled flights that reduce international transportation times to as little as one or two days. FedEx, UPS, and others have also entered the market, offering door-to-door delivery and other logistical services. High-dollar, low-weight items are still most commonly moved by air.

International airlines are subject to various government regulations. Regulation between any two countries is still relatively strict in most cases. Movements may be governed by *bilateral agreements*—contracts between two countries to allow air service. For the United States, these agreements are negotiated between the Office of International Aviation and the U.S. Department of State. Specific airports, a carrier from each nation to provide service on the route, and the amount of service to be provided are negotiated in advance between the two countries. The United States also has negotiated "open-skies" agreements with more than 100 countries, which allow free access to the other countries' international air markets and multilateral agreements with others such as the European Union (U.S. Department of State, 2021).

Intermodalism

Intermodalism is important in the international movement of freight. *Intermodalism* refers to the movement of containers (one mode) using at least one other mode of transportation. A multimodal bill of lading, or combined transport bill of lading, may be used to cover the multiple movements, thus decreasing the amount of paperwork.

The options to shippers include:

- all water transportation;
- *mini land bridge*;
- *land bridge*; and
- *micro-bridge.*

A mini land bridge, or *mini-bridge*, is the shipment of goods from one country's port to a second country's port, with overland transportation in the first country. For example, a shipment may originate from a port in Long Beach, California, move across the United States via rail to New York, and then move via ship to its final destination of La Havre, France. A *land bridge* is a shipment between two countries, with overland transportation in a third country. For example, goods are shipped from Shanghai, China, to Rotterdam, Netherlands, via the United States, where the containers are unloaded in Seattle, Washington, and transported via air to New York City, and then on to Rotterdam. Lastly, a *micro-bridge* is a shipment from one country's port to another country's inland destination or vice versa. For example, containers are shipped from Da Nang to Dallas via San Francisco, where they are loaded onto rail cars for transportation to their final destination.

Intermediaries

A number of third parties, or intermediaries, are important to the successful shipment of goods from one country to another. *Foreign freight forwarders* are a good option for those new to international buying. They hire people with expertise in all areas of global shipping to help those organizations too small to have a department devoted to international issues. Foreign freight forwarders typically consolidate small shipments into container-size lots or to fill an entire ship. They also play a needed role in advising shippers on the best means to package and ship goods, as well as how to assure their shipment meets all statutory and maritime obligations (Farrow, 2021). DHL, Schenker and C.H. Robinson are just a few of the many companies that offer freight forwarding services. Their fees are earned through document preparation or commissions charged to carriers. They also perform other functions, including:

- rate quotes;
- document preparation;
- chartering/booking vessels;
- obtaining cargo insurance;
- customs clearance;
- paying freight charges;
- tracing/expediting shipments;
- language translation; and
- arranging for inland transportation service.

(Coyle et al., 1996)

An *air freight forwarder* performs similar functions to a foreign freight forwarder, but for air freight only. It may prepare and present documentation, trace and expedite shipments, publish tariffs, issue air waybills, and accept responsibility for damaged shipments.

Non-vessel-operating common carriers focus on the consolidation of small shipments into containers headed to inland destinations. They will book container space on steamship liners at reduced rates and then resell that space to small shippers, giving them the price advantage of being a large shipper. Since the passage of OSRA, U.S.-owned NVOCCs must be licensed. They must file a bond or provide proof of financial responsibility in an amount determined by the FMC.

Shippers' associations are another means of moving small shipments for members through consolidation. As nonprofit cooperatives, these associations can negotiate lower rates because of the larger volume shipments and pass those rates on to members. Members also avoid the markups charged by the other intermediaries mentioned earlier. Because members are acting collectively, they generally receive better service from carriers.

Customs house brokers, licensed by the U.S. Department of the Treasury, provide a service to shippers by assuring all documentation required for a shipment is complete and accurate for entrance into the United States. The advent of computers has made their job much easier, reducing the time needed for clearance through Customs and thus reducing overall lead times on international shipments.

Ship brokers are sales and marketing representatives for charter vessel owners, acting as middlemen between ship owners and shippers. A ship broker keeps track of port calls or when ships will be in port, and then matches this with the needs of a shipper.

Ship agents represent the vessel owner while the ship is in port. The agent arranges for several things, including the ship's arrival, berthing, any clearances needed, unloading and loading, and payment of port fees.

Terms of Sale and Documentation

Terms of sale include when and where the actual transfer of goods (i.e., trade terms), payment, legal title, and responsibility for insuring the goods take place. The trade terms most widely used internationally are known as Incoterms®, were first published by the International Chamber of Commerce in Paris in 1936 and most recently revised in 2020 (ICC, 2021). They provide a set of uniform rules for international transactions, including defining the risks, costs, and obligations of both buyer and seller. While not law, Incoterms® should be included in the contract to avoid future misunderstandings and disputes. If there are disputes, the courts or arbitrators will use the sales contract as one point of reference in addition to whoever has possession of the goods and whether payment has been made. There are 11 rules grouped into two categories. The first group of seven rules applies to any mode or modes of transport, while the second group consists of four rules for sea and inland water transport only. The most commonly used rules used by government agencies would likely be "Delivered at Place" (DAP), "Cost and Freight" (CFR) and "Cost, Insurance and Freight" (CIF). *DAP* indicates the seller is responsible for all costs for delivery of goods to a designated location. *CFR* means the seller will pay the transportation costs and deliver the goods to a designated port; while *CIF* requires the seller to also pay for marine insurance. More detailed information can be found on the ICC website (https://iccwbo.org/).

Documentation specific to international shipments is also common when importing goods into the United States and can be overwhelming, requiring absolute accuracy to avoid shipment delays. Government and industry are both working to simplify the process, thereby reducing transaction costs and time. For example, the United States-Mexico-Canada Trade Agreement "ensures data can be transferred across borders" and "facilitates digital transactions" such as electronic authentication and electronic signatures" (USMCA, 2021). With the increased use of electronic solutions, the need for paper documents has diminished. U.S. Customs has also streamlined the process with a completely paperless environment. It uses the Automated Manifest System by which shippers may notify Customs of inbound air, sea, or rail shipments before they arrive at a U.S. point of entry using electronic data interchange

(EDI) or a portal. Customs then notifies shippers as to which ones need to be inspected, and those shipments can be designated before arrival, thus speeding up the process. Once the goods are inspected, they receive electronic clearance. The Automated Brokerage Interface also is available, which allows messaging between U.S. Customs and intermediaries to facilitate a shipment's clearance.

In addition to the shipping documentation required, *letters of credit* are important in international transactions, protecting both the buyer and seller. A letter of credit, also known as *documentary credit*, is a bank's written promise to pay the seller on behalf of the buyer for goods purchased. The bank acts as an intermediary, collecting payment from the buyer and forwarding it to the seller once proof is presented that the goods have been shipped. The buyer is then entitled to the goods upon arrival. A bill of lading provides evidence of shipment and title transfer. Using a fictional example, the City of Dayton, located in Ohio, wants to purchase concrete pumps from Lassie Industries, located in Ireland. The City of Dayton and Lassie Industries have negotiated the price, delivery time, and other terms; but Lassie Industries is not willing to ship the equipment without being paid in advance, and does not want to ship cash on delivery because of fears that the equipment may be rejected. The City of Dayton's procurement professional has never had dealings with Lassie Industries and does not want to pay in advance. As a result, the City of Dayton has its bank issue a letter of credit. The letter states that the bank will honor a draft drawn against the bank in the agreed amount. The draft must include specified documents, such as the bill of lading, the signed commercial invoice, packing documents, and insurance forms.

Packaging, Labeling, and Marking

Because internationally purchased goods are in transit longer and handled more frequently, they are more susceptible to damage from poor weather conditions. Packaging is an important protection but can add costs to global versus domestic movements through the use of more material and labor. Today, there is also pressure to use sustainable packaging and then recycle that packaging. Labeling and marking requirements vary from country to country and are an additional expense. In the United States, there is no one law or agency that oversees labeling, so it is a good idea to do some research to assure all requirements are met in order to avoid fines and penalties. Labeling is regulated to provide product descriptions through set standards, enforce compliance with current product standards, and restrict or control the use of additives. Marking helps facilitate package identification through the use of certain numbers, letters, and symbols. Marking may include weight, height, invoice numbers, and transit instructions. In the United States, Control and Border Protection (CBP) is responsible for establishing and enforcing marking requirements.

Ports

The points where shipments are exchanged between water and land carriers are referred to as *ports*. They serve several functions, as listed in Figure 6.5. *Container ports* are often part of a larger port. There also are *smart ports*, which use advanced technologies such as AI, big data, IoT and blockchain to enhance performance.

Twenty-five U.S. ports served hundreds of ships in 2019, handling about 1.82 billion tons of cargo, which accounted for 77% of total freight tons. Additionally, containers at the 25 largest ports moved 55.5 billion TEUs that same year—about 95% of total TEUs (U.S. Department of Transportation, 2020). The volume of trade grew more than 10% from 2009 through 2019 (United States Bureau of Transportation, 2021). Most cargo entering the United States is transferred to rail or truck for transport to its final destination. However, congestion at the marine terminal gate is a challenge in the nation's busiest ports. Most of these problems occur because of truck and rail access to the terminal area. For railroads, bridge clearance or the distance from the railroad to the terminal may cause such problems. For trucks, roads connecting marine terminals with the national highway system often are inadequate.

There are other challenges as well. Port operations, in general, affect air quality and land use. As a result, ports are looking to invest in cleaner technologies. Workforce issues are another issue, forcing ports to adopt technologies

Figure 6.5 Port functions

Discharging the ship to shore
Mooring ships
Checking goods for quality, correct quantity, legal entry
Sorting goods for shipment
Storage
Assessing duties
Loading containers onto vehicles such as trucks and trains
Moving goods from dock area to transportation network

where possible to increase capacity. However, these changes require additional worker training and the resolution of workforce union issues. Lastly, container shipping has grown significantly, but repositioning empty containers until they can be used again is always an issue. The cost of moving and storing containers can be more than the value of the container. Also, some ports are too small to handle the demand for containers (United States Environmental Protection Agency, 2021).

There is also the issue of securing U.S. ports against terrorist attacks. The Port and Maritime Security Act of 2002 was enacted to do just this. The Act identifies the responsibilities of several agencies, including the following:

- U.S. Coast Guard: Ensures the safety and security of U.S. maritime interests and leads homeland security efforts.
- CBP: Screens "incoming vessels' crew and maritime cargo for the presence of contraband" (GAO, 2012).
- Transportation Security Administration: Manages the Transportation Worker Identification Credential Program.
- Domestic Nuclear Detection Office: Acquires and supports "the deployment of radiation detection equipment ... to support the scanning of cargo containers before they enter the U.S" (GAO, 2012).
- Federal Emergency Management Agency: Administers "grants to improve the security of the nation's highest risk port areas" (GAO, 2012).

Conclusions

Procurement professionals are increasingly buying in global markets and must thus consider related transportation issues. Recent trends indicate that the amount of global trade should continue to increase for the foreseeable future. There are multiple components of global transportation that do not fall within the procurement professional's control, including infrastructure, legal, cultural differences, and political climate. The procurement professional should consider these issues and others when buying transportation services. Intermediaries—including foreign freight forwarders and customs brokers, among others—can make these transactions easier.

References

Anonymous, "Connectivity, Logistics & Trade Facilitation," The World Bank. www.worldbank.org/en/topic/trade-facilitation-and-logistics.

Anonymous (2021). "What is a Vessel Sharing Agreement (VSA) in Shipping?" E-Ports. www.e-ports.com/regulations/ce0aee96f73a48a48f4bcc460b5ccc23.
Brett, D. (2021), "Air Cargo Gains from Rising Prices in Ocean Shipping," Air Cargo News, July 14. www.aircargonews.net/business/airfreight-rates/air-cargo-gains-from-rising-prices-in-ocean-shipping/.
Branch, A.E. (1989). *Elements of Shipping* (6th ed.) London: Chapman and Hall.
Coyle, J. J., Bardi, E. J., & Langley, C. J., Jr. (1996). *The Management of Business Logistics* (6th ed.). Minneapolis/St. Paul, MN: West Publishing Company.
U.S. Department of State (2021). "Open Skies Agreements." https://2009-2017.state.gov/e/eb/tra/ata/index.htm.
Farrow (2021). "What is Freight Forwarding?" https://farrow.com/resources/what-is-freight-forwarding/.
Frese, F. (2019). "Shipping Alliances: 2M, Ocean Alliance and THE Alliance," July 31. https://container-xchange.com/blog/shipping-alliances/.
GAO (2012). "Maritime Security: Progress and Challenges 10 Years after the Maritime Transportation Security Act," November 11. www.gao.gov/assets/gao-12-1009t.pdf.
Gourdin, K. N. (2001). *Global Logistics Management.* Oxford, UK: Blackwell Publishers, Ltd.
Hall, R. D. (1992). *International Trade Operations* (2nd ed.). Jersey City, NJ: Unz and Company.
Harrington, L. H. (1999). "A new era dawns," Industry Week, January 5.
Hartman, F. (2021). "EU-Mercosur Free Trade Agreement," Royal Institute, May 25. https://blog.realinstitutoelcano.org/en/eu-mercosur-free-trade-agreement/.
ICC (2021). "Incoterms® 2020." https://iccwbo.org/resources-for-business/incoterms-rules/incoterms-2020/.
Kharpal, A. (2021). "How Asia came to Dominate Chip-making and what the U.S. wants to do about it, CNBC, April 11. www.cnbc.com/2021/04/12/us-semiconductor-policy-looks-to-cut-out-china-secure-supply-chain.html.
Kroll, K. (2020). "TMS Put to the Test," Inbound Logistics, August 24. www.inbound-logistics.com/cms/article/put-to-the-test/.
Miller, G. (2021). "No Relief: Global Container Shortage Likely to Last Until 2022," Freightwaves, April 30. www.freightwaves.com/news/no-relief-global-container-shortage-likely-to-last-until-2022.
Office of the United States Trade Representative (2020), "United States-Mexico-Canada Trade Agreement." https://ustr.gov/trade-agreements/free-trade-agreements/united-states-mexico-canada-agreement.
Ronconi, L. (2019). "Enforcement of Labor Regulations in Developing Countries, IZA World of Labor. https://wol.iza.org/articles/enforcement-of-labor-regulations-in-developing-countries/long.
Statista (2021). "Container Shipping – Statistics & Facts," September 23. www.statista.com/topics/1367/container-shipping/#dossierKeyfigures.
Supply Chain Quarterly Staff (2015). "Sourcing Internationally: Six Risks and How to Mitigate Them," Supply Chain Quarterly, May 27. www.supplychainquarterly.com/articles/984-sourcing-internationally-six-risks-and-how-to-mitigate-them.

Tradelens (2021), "Hapag-Lloyd and Ocean Network Express Complete Tradelens Integration," June 21. www.tradelens.com/post/hapag-lloyd-and-ocean-network-express-complete-tradelens-integration.

UNCTAD (2021). "Global Trade Update," May. https://unctad.org/system/files/official-document/ditcinf2021d2_en.pdf.

U.S. Census Bureau, Foreign Trade Division (2021). "U.S. International Trade in Goods and Services." www.census.gov/foreign-trade/statistics/historical/index.html.

U.S. Department of Transportation (2020). "Port Performance Freight Statistics Annual Report to Congress 2020." https://rosap.ntl.bts.gov/view/dot/54022.

U.S. Department of Transportation (2021). "Tonnage of Top 50 U.S. Water Ports, Ranked by Total Tons." www.bts.gov/content/tonnage-top-50-us-water-ports-ranked-total-tons.

USMCA. "Digital Trade." https://ustr.gov/sites/default/files/files/Press/fs/USMCA/USMCA-Digital_Trade.pdf.

United States Environmental Protection Agency (2021). "Ports Primer: 2.2 Current Port Industry Challenges," July 15. www.epa.gov/community-port-collaboration/ports-primer-22-current-port-industry-challenges.

Wackett, Mike (2021). "Port of Durban Recovers from Civil Unrest but Citrus Industry Feels Long-Term Pain," July 20. https://theloadstar.com/port-of-durban-recovers-from-civil-unrest-but-citrus-industry-feels-long-term-pain/.

World Bank (2021). "Global Preferential Trade Agreements Database." https://wits.worldbank.org/gptad/trade_database.html.

World Trade Organization (2021). "Who We Are." https://www.wto.org/english/thewto_e/whatis_e/who_we_are_e.htm

Zhao, J. (2019), "Environmental Regulations: Lessons for Developing Economies in Asia," July, ADBI Working Paper Services #980. Tokyo: Asian Development Bank Institute.

Chapter 7

Technology in the Supply Chain

Introduction

As procurement and supply professionals continue to move away from simply processing transactions to a more strategic role of managing supplier relationships, the view of the entity becomes one of an *extended enterprise* of buyers, suppliers, intermediaries, and transportation carriers. Multiple entities must be strategically aligned, focusing on specific market opportunities. Shared information among these individual entities makes this concept of the extended enterprise and a true supply chain possible. Linking procurement directly to suppliers and transportation carriers allows for "real-time" responses to changes in market conditions. Availability of information also aids decision making, helps reduce costs, and increases the responsiveness of a transportation network. Simply stated, information systems allow for planning, control, and matching of supply with demand in short timeframes. Today, digital software, hardware, the Internet, and other tools make information sharing a reality.

Rethinking the Supply Chain and Information

A common visual conception of the supply chain is the *link-and-mode model.* Over the years, many have viewed supply chains as a variety of sequential steps that are linked to one another. The reality, however, is that supply chains must

DOI: 10.4324/9781003298625-7

be truly integrated to be successfully managed. While supply chain activities and players remain consistent, today's leaders stress the importance of a truly integrated approach. Each link must be connected with the others across a network of upstream and downstream activities (Mangan et al, 2012). Figure 7.1 depicts a view of a modern, integrated supply chain. The flow of materials is important, but so is the flow of information. This will best allow resources to be managed effectively by supply chain professionals.

Several shipments from suppliers, for example, can be synchronized to arrive at the same time as required by the customer. Additionally, the customer, supplier, transportation carrier, and other intermediaries can regularly monitor information on the status of an order or shipment. Essentially, this is a movement beyond EDI to an electronic network of simultaneous connections with all partners necessary to transact business. From this connectivity comes something referred to as *economies of conjunction*, or the efficiencies and speed that are possible based on how entities manage information and business transaction. Economies of conjunction can be extended to logistics (Stock, Greis & Kasarda, 2000). Research suggests that entities should strive to develop a "logistics environment" which is time sensitive, flexible, and collaborative. This environment is now possible because of real-time movement of information among partnering entities. To achieve this, entities need a transportation network consisting of multiple modes capable of moving products and materials without interruption based on client requirements. A network of multimodal and intermodal transportation requires information access. All partners require electronic connectivity to access a shared information network.

Figure 7.1 The integrated supply chain

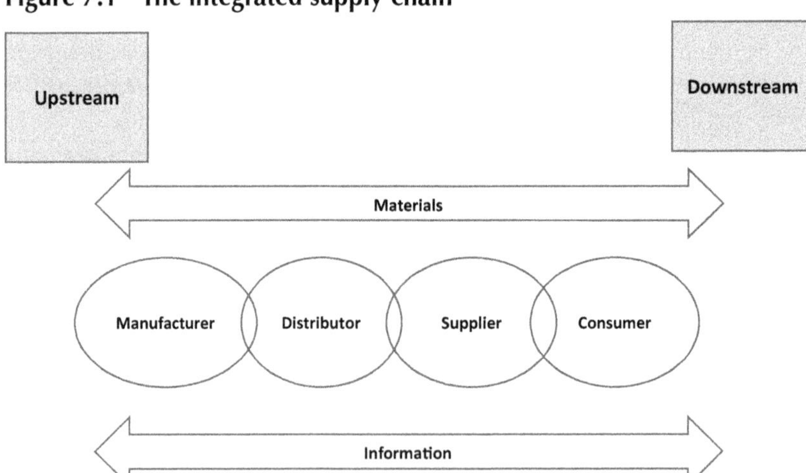

Current Issues in Technology

A 2021 research report from Accenture resulted in some interesting findings related to technology and supply chain management (Accenture, 2021). Over 600 supply chain executives were surveyed from leading organizations around the world in a variety of sectors. Supply chain leaders shared their perspectives on technology priorities, how technology could reshape the supply chain, and the impacts that these technologies would have on their respective organizations. A summary of some key findings can be found in Figure 7.2.

This study indicates that organizations realize the value of technology and are willing to make the necessary investments to ensure an effective and efficient supply chain. It also appears that supply chain leaders do not believe their procurement and supply chain staff are necessarily ready for cutting-edge technology, but that leaders are willing to invest in them to ensure they will be.

The top issues for supply chain leaders, according to Accenture, are the use of cloud technology (42%) and AI (36%), which are both addressed later in this chapter.

CIPS, based in the United Kingdom, offers some insights into the top technology trends in the field. The top five technology trends, as identified by CIPS, are as follows:

- integrating a digital transformation strategy;
- adopting AI systems;

Figure 7.2 Technology and supply chains

Finding	*Percentage Agreed*
The COVID-19 pandemic has been the organization's largest stress test.	81
Organizations are facing technological changes at an unprecedented speed and scale.	81
Organizations believe their workforce is ready to leverage the technology tools they are given.	38
Organizations plan to invest in employees that do not have the requisite expertise in technology.	78
Multiparty systems will become the center of commerce, supply chain, and transactions among partners and customers.	87
Organizations will conduct over 50% of their business in the Cloud over the next three years.	93

Source: Accenture (2021). Tech Vision 2021: The technology trends which will shape the future.

- focusing on cybersecurity systems and protection;
- using big data to drive decisions; and
- adopting block chain infrastructure and transactions.

(CIPS, 2019)

Software applications continue to advance and offer a variety of robust features to supply chain professionals in all areas. Leading providers vie for market share in all sectors and industries, offering platforms that can bring efficiency to all areas of procurement and supply chain management. The following is a list of some of the most common applications:

- transportation management systems;
- inventory control and forecasting;
- digital procurement;
- contract management;
- warehouse management; and
- customer relationship management.

It is not unusual for supply chain managers to use multiple systems to manage their operations, although many platforms offer multiple modules that can address different areas of the supply chain. For example, Oracle offers a solution that includes both procurement (e.g., supplier registration, sourcing, offer evaluation) and warehouse management (e.g., inventory control, reordering, forecasting) features (www.oracle.com/erp/procurement-cloud).

IT Today

There are multiple means to stay connected in the supply chain. While EDI has been around for many years, the Internet has rapidly grown as a means of communication among supply chain partners.

Electronic Data Interchange

EDI, a staple in communications technology, is defined as the electronic transfer and exchange of business documents between organizations using networks and the Internet (NIGP, 2021). Introduced in the 1970s, EDI improves the speed and accuracy of paper-based documents. In recent decades, the use of EDI has increased rapidly. The benefits of EDI include improved cash flows, productivity, and supplier diversity, with reductions in the following areas:

- document preparation;
- inventory on hand;
- personnel costs;
- order lead times;
- processing time;
- carrying costs;
- shipping errors; and
- ordering costs.

(Sabatino, 2020)

Transportation companies use EDI to replace paper shipping documents, including freight bills, bills of lading, shipment status, pickup requests, and remittance advices.

Internet

As noted many years ago by Christopher (1998: 272), "The Internet provides a perfect vehicle for the establishment of the virtual supply chain." A recent study found that long-haul truck drivers can certainly benefit from its

Figure 7.3 EDI applications

Area	*Use*
General industry	Inventory control, purchase orders, and supplier invoices are examples of industry transactions that use EDI.
Financial sector	The financial sector can use this technology for things like insurance management, verifying account balances, and determining interest rates.
Transportation	All types of data within the supply chain can be accessed through EDI, which includes key areas of the transportation industry.
Automotive	Manufacturers in the automotive industry may use this technology to exchange information on vehicle designs, as well as sharing information within a company.
Health iIndustry	Within the health and medical sector, information such as claims, patient eligibility, and general health reports can be accessed through this technology.

Source: Adapted from Map My EDI (2020). Will the Advantages of EDI Hold True in the Future? https://mapmyedi.com/knowledge-base/advantages-of-edi/.

use. These drivers experience unpredictable schedules, long periods of travel, and a sense of social isolation, making the Internet an ideal resource. While the research found that Internet use was limited for many drivers, practical uses included access to roadmaps, locations of fuel stops, and transmission of documents. Unsurprisingly, the age and experience of the drivers also played a role in their use of the Internet. Older and more experienced drivers reported lower use than younger drivers, who are likely more accustomed to using a variety of web applications (Heaton, Combs & Griffin, 2017).

After conducting a study of 22 motor carriers, KPMG International designed a model to categorize carriers based on their Internet use. Four stages of Internet usage were identified:

- marketing basic information, including breadth of services;
- publishing pricing information and annual reports;
- creating two-way transactional flows with customers/partners, including information access, placing, and changing orders; and
- conducting all business transactions and information sharing with real-time shipment visibility, collaborative planning, and customer order management.

The research found that most carriers fell into the third category above (KPMG, 2000). Frequently offered services include freight quotes, shipment tracking, pickup scheduling, and access to receipts or bills of lading, which streamline and cut costs from the typical shipment. While the company may have access, the traffic department may not. Therefore, many freight companies are looking to alternative systems that include extension of the Internet, including extranets and intranets.

Technology will continue to enhance the efficiency of the transportation industry. Knowing where a truck is in transit can be invaluable to suppliers and customers that are waiting on shipments. This is sometimes referred to as the "Amazon effect," since consumers are accustomed to knowing exactly where their goods are and when they will arrive. Carriers of all sizes are utilizing these technologies to stay competitive. These electronic tools help with matching trucks to available loads, as well as providing updates on billing and payment status (Lockridge, 2019).

Extranets

Extranets are defined as "an extension of the corporate Intranet that uses web technology to improve communication with its suppliers and customers, providing limited access to increase the speed and efficiency of their business relationship" (Bagci, 2020). An extranet has the advantage of opening up company information to customers and partners. CSX Corporation, a leading transportation provider in the United States and Canada, uses extranet technology to communicate shipping information to its customers in real time. Customers can easily determine the feasibility of rail transit, obtain pricing information, or look up rail schedules (www.csx.com). With a railway-based service that serves 23 states and the provinces of Ontario and Quebec, CSX believes that, through the use of leading technology, it can improve the pace and quality of decision making (Stagl, 2021).

Intranets

With many organizations opening up information access through extranets, transportation companies are also placing a high priority on intranets. An *intranet* has been described as "a private network inside a company or organization built by using Internet technologies" (NIGP, 2021). Intranets provide information sharing with access to text-based documents and corporate databases from any desktop with a browser. Yellow Transportation, Inc., a Fortune 500 holding corporation for a family of companies specializing in freight transportation, uses its intranet to provide its terminal operating system, which shares operations best practices and provides forums, bulletin boards, and online chats.

American Airlines utilizes an interactive intranet to increase engagement and alignment between corporate leaders and employees. With over 100,000 employees, the airline can engage in meaningful conversations by using the Jive platform. Rank-and-file staff can share their insights and ideas, while senior leadership can better communicate the company's vision and values (Jive, 2021).

There are some drawbacks to intranets. Information is available in a multitude of sources and in all kinds of formats. Published documents may also be presented in an unstructured way. As a result, finding relevant and accurate information may be difficult, requiring a search through several systems. Information can be accessed through different methods, including web browsers, email systems, and other software applications. These applications may integrate with online databases, such as enterprise resource planning or customer relationship management platforms.

As a result, more organizations are moving toward exchange portals, which improve access to needed information. Exchange portals—web interfaces to an organizational network—organize information into content-specific areas to improve communication. There also are industry-based portals, which are used to promote communication among supply partners within a specific industry. For example, the automotive industry has created an exchange portal to exchange information on designs, bids, schedules, and commodities (Northeast Automotive Alliance).

Wireless Technology

Wireless computing provides a mobile platform, which is ideal in the logistics and transportation industry. Local and regional delivery companies can use wireless technology to track packages, while trucking and transportation companies track vehicles and goods. For example, the Global Positioning System (GPS) is the basis for locating fleet vehicles in the trucking industry. Motor carriers can modify their routes based on the nearest available truck to improve customer response time. Rail companies are using wireless computing to improve scheduling of services and send arrival and departure information. R&L Carriers, with a fleet of 21,000 tractors and trailers, serves multiple states and provinces across the United States, Canada, and Puerto Rico (www.rlcarriers.com). It uses a portable document capture system that includes a scanner, computer, and wireless access. Drivers submit shipping documents or bills of lading to corporate headquarters in real time for immediate processing. Bills for shipments can be generated within a day versus a week under the old system. Shipment information is also posted on the company website, which allows customers and shippers continuous access to tracking data. Transit times, service maps, and shipment status are available whenever needed.

Remote Control Technology

To improve safety, Class I railroads in the United States have begun pilot testing remote control technology, which utilizes an onboard computer to operate locomotives based on signals received from ground employees. In the past, a ground employee directed traffic via radio or hand signals to the locomotive engineer. The Canadian National Railroad has used remote control technology for many years, and yard accidents have been reduced significantly. Known as *positive train control*, the technology supports the safe and efficient operation of remote-control locomotives. Based on research conducted by Transport Canada, guidelines have been established on the qualification and training of operators to reduce the risk of incidents (Transport Canada, 2019).

Remote-control technology also can be used in warehouses to operate forklifts. Referred to as *teleoperation*, drivers are equipped with joysticks, steering wheels, and pedals at their computer screen. This allows them to safely operate a forklift from a different building or even from home (Baraniuk, 2020). Teleoperation is also being used to remotely control delivery trucks. In some instances, the truck may not even have a cab or manual controls, which allows it to haul more freight. A human still operates the truck but does so in front of a computer screen and controls that can be several miles away (Carpenter, 2018).

Barcoding

Barcodes, read by optical scanners, have had a major impact on logistics since the 1970s. Used to identify incoming shipments, barcodes consist of a series of parallel black and white bars of varying width. The sequence translates into letters or numbers that represent information, including the shipment's origin, product type, place of manufacture, and product price (Coyle, Bardi, & Langley, 1996). Each industry has its own barcode standards, which include the code "language," print quality, type of information included, and information format. The lack of common standards across industries is one of the biggest issues facing organizations.

Scanners emit light beams to read the barcodes and may be stationary, hand-held, or attached to the wrist or finger. The advantages of scanning include improved data accuracy, reduced receiving time, and integration of data with inventory controls, and databases.

Radio Frequency

Radio frequency (RF) is used to relay information between drivers or operators and a warehouse or port yard. Radio frequency identification (RFID) identifies trailers, tractors, or other equipment in a yard; monitors trailer status at a remote location; and identifies arriving and departing tractors and trailers at yard gates. RF data collection is used to communicate with the driver or other mobile personnel. RF tags are programmed with content information for each container of ammunition. Tagging allows an organization to track containers and review the tag periodically at the port of departure, holding yards, the port of destination, and the final arrival point to determine what is in a container. Barcodes also are attached to the shipment to notify the shipper that a container has been loaded.

RFID technology provides information and visibility in real time. It can be used by an organization across the supply chain to do things like trigger production or the movement of freight. It can also reduce logistical costs, as it helps to minimize inventory and resource requirements (Mangan et al, 2012). The primary applications and benefits of RFID include:

- asset tracking and management;
- increased security of freight;
- improved stock management and availability; and
- reduced errors in product data handling.

Artificial Intelligence

AI allows computers and machines to function in an intelligent manner. It is a system that can interpret and correct external data, and has the potential to replace human labor for certain tasks. A common view of AI is that it can help humans solve problems and facilitate work processes, including those related to supply chain management. AI is intelligence designed by humans and demonstrated by machines (Tai, 2020). The impact of AI in logistics management is far reaching. Areas such as terminal management, inbound logistics and transportation system automation are just a few examples (Toorajipou, et al, 2021).

Internet of Things

In recent years, much attention has been paid to IoT. It has an impact on how people travel and shop, how manufacturers keep track of inventory, and so much more. IoT is the concept of connecting any electronic device to the Internet and to other connected devices. In this huge network of connected people, things, and information, individuals have access to data that enables them to make sound decisions. It could be an alarm clock adjusting a wakeup time upon a later train schedule and inclement weather, or a connected transport vehicle with a check engine light that notifies the manufacturer and local dealer of a needed repair (Clark, 2016).

Blockchain

Blockchain is a relatively new concept in supply chain management and is referred to by some as an *online ledger*. Blockchain is a growing list of records (or blocks) that are linked using cryptography. Each block contains information on transaction data and a timestamp, and is by design resistant to modification. Like other online systems, blockchain is subject to cyberattacks and therefore enhanced security measures are employed. Blockchain creates a record of transactions that cannot be altered and does so with end-to-end encryption. This is meant to eliminate fraud and unauthorized activities. Data on the blockchain is held across a network of computers in the hope of making it nearly impossible to hack. Before a block of transactions can be made part of the blockchain, the parties must agree to the transaction as valid. This is done through a process referred to as *consensus* (www.blockchain-council.org).

Cloud Computing

Valuable data files are commonly stored in the cloud, which can consist of multiple locations or data centers that house the information. While the needed data might not reside within an organization, with proper credentials it can easily access its information when needed. Common examples of cloud computing include the recording of a video meeting on Zoom or the storage of personal photos from a smartphone. More and more providers of software as a services work with supply chain customers and host their systems and data in the cloud. This can include systems for transportation management, sourcing, contract management, and others.

Drone Delivery

Technology has been around for several years that allows a drone to deliver a package from a distribution center to a customer by air. Drones use rotors for liftoff as well as navigation in all directions needed to make a delivery. The advantages of drones include quicker delivery and reduced traffic on the roadways.

Many companies are now investing in drone technology in the belief that it will have an increased role in transportation in the future. UPS has developed a program that has drones using the delivery truck as a liftoff point. One of the largest logistics companies in the world, DHL, recently partnered with drone specialist DHang to deliver small packages in China (Kumar, 2019). These are great examples of what is possible with drone technology, but the extent of their use moving forward has yet to be determined.

Global Positioning System

Originally developed by the U.S. government, GPS can let a person know exactly where they are on Earth. Through the use of satellites, GPS can also inform how far away a destination is and the expected time of arrival (Library of Congress, 2019). Its use can include the tracking of wildlife or the resolution of property boundary disputes, but of course it also has applications in transportation management. GPS is a proven technology for navigation including air, water, and ground carriers using GPS receivers. Additionally, it can be useful for vehicle tracking and route planning for goods and materials.

Robotics

The use of robots continues to increase in logistics and warehousing. Loading and unloading of trucks, movement of materials throughout the warehouse, and order picking are just some of the common uses. Warehouse employees often work in conjunction with a robot (a cobot rather than a coworker) to perform routine tasks. When robots are used in logistical operations, they can handle a variety of repeatable movements over long periods of time. On average, a robot is twice as productive as a human performing the same task (Sakharkar, 2021). Robot automation in the supply chain will continue in the future as technology advances. It can be viewed as a valuable augmentation to human labor.

Case Study: Robotic Retrieval System

Santa Clara University in California has plenty of room in its campus library for reading and studying. With all the couches and open spaces, a visitor might wonder where all the books are located.

The inventory of 800,000 books and library items resides in an automated retrieval system. This is a robot-operated storage facility two stories tall. When a patron requests a book, robotic cranes move to the appropriate metal bin, retrieve the item, and deliver it to the operator in about five minutes. Customer service is still provided by humans, however.

Source: Santa Clara University, www.scu.edu; and Court Mann, "Santa Clara University library assisted by giant robots", The Daily Universe, June 20, 2011.

Planning for Technology

Transportation companies are searching for new technologies that will increase their productivity and improve customer service. A multitude of product offerings are available, making the choices challenging for both carrier and customer. To evaluate the information technology decision, various factors should be considered, including the following:

- What are the entity's requirements regarding transportation?
- How will the technology improve coordination of key logistics activities?
- What is the timeline for meeting the implementation goals?
- How will business continuity be ensured during implementation?
- How will effectiveness be monitored and evaluated?
- What training strategies will be used?
- How will funding be provided?

(Stanley, 2014)

As in other areas of supply chain management, transportation and logistics activities should be well thought out as part of a strategic plan. This should include participation by all stakeholders in an entity to ensure the smooth implementation of new technology. While each entity is unique, the involvement of the procurement, supply chain management, finance, IT, and risk management functions is common.

Conclusions

Significant advances have been made to improve communication within an entity and among supply chain partners. Advances in technology have reduced uncertainties in the supply chain, making it easier to exchange information and track the movement of goods. A good information system will assist in the planning and decision-making process, but should be designed with an entity's specific needs in mind. While there have been major advances in technology in recent years, there are still opportunities for future improvements in performance through supply chain analysis techniques. Technology should be viewed as a powerful tool by supply chain professionals, as it can provide the necessary information to make sound decisions for their entity. Rather than viewing advancing technology as a threat to take over routine tasks, it can be viewed as an opportunity to increase the value and efficiency of supply chain management.

References

Accenture (2021). "Tech Vision 2021: The technology trends which will shape the future." www.accenture.com/us-en/insights/technology/technology-trends-2021.

Bagci, T. (2020). "What is an Extranet?" Sysnettech Solutions, October. www.sysnettech solutions.com/en/what-is-extranet/.

Baraniuk, C. (2020). "The forklift truck drivers that never leave their desks," BBC News, Business, October 20. www.bbc.com/news/business-54431056.

Carpenter, S. (2018). "Remote Controlled Trucks Moving from Toy Shelves to the Open Road," Trucks, August 2. www.trucks.com/2018/08/02/remote-controlled-trucks/.

Christopher, M. (1998). *Logistics and Supply Chain Management*. London, UK: Prentice Hall.

Clark, J. (2016). "What is the Internet of Things?" IBM Business Operations Blog, November 17. www.ibm.com/blogs/internet-of-things/what-is-the-iot/.

Coyle, J. J., Bardi, E. J., & Langley, C. J., Jr. (1996). *The Management of Business Logistics* (6th ed.). Minneapolis/St. Paul, MN: West Publishing Company.

CSX. (2002). "CSXT introduces remote control technology." www.csx.com.

Davydov, M. M. (2001). *Corporate Portals and E-business Integration*. New York: McGraw Hill.

Emmelhainz, M. A. (1992). *EDI: A Total Management Guide*. London, UK: International Thomson Computer Press.

Hannon, D. (2001). "Logistics and the Internet: Internet connections make shipments more visible," Purchasing Today, November 15.

Heaton, K., Combs, B. and Griffin, R. (2017). "Truck Drivers' Use of the Internet: A Mobile Health Lifeline," Workplace Health and Safety, June.

Johnson, J. C., Wood, D. F., Wardlow, D. L., & Murphy P. R., Jr. (1999). *Contemporary Logistics*. Upper Saddle River, NJ: Prentice Hall.

KPMG International. (2000). *Strategic Directions in E-Transportation*. New York: KPMG LLP

Kumar, A. (2019). "Drone Delivery – Future of Shipping Industry", Circuit Digest, September 3. https://circuitdigest.com/article/drone-delivery-future-of-shipping-industry.

Lamber, F. (2021). "Elon Musk's Boring Company 'Tesla in Tunnels' in Las Vegas to expand throughout the city," Electrek, October 20. https://electrek.co/2021/10/20/elon-musk-boring-company-tesla-in-tunnels-las-vegas-expand/.

Lockridge, D. (2019). "Technology is Changing How Carriers, Shippers and Brokers Connect," Trucking Info, July 17. www.truckinginfo.com/336365/technology-is-changing-how-carriers-shippers-and-brokers-connect.

Mangan, J., Lalwani, C., Butcher, T. & Javadpour, R. (2012). *Global Logistics and Supply Chain Management*. Chichester, UK: John Wiley & Sons Ltd.

NIGP: The Institute for Public Procurement (2021). *Public Procurement Dictionary of Terms*. Herndon, VA: NIGP. www.nigp.org.

Northeast Automotive Alliance, Procurement, NEAA Procurement Portland. https://northeastautomotivealliance.com/automotive-sector/

Sabatino, A. (2020). "Realizing the Benefits of the New EDI," Supply Chain Brain, Think Tank, July 10. www.supplychainbrain.com/blogs/1-think-tank/post/31558-realizing-the-benefits-of-the-new-edi.

Sakharkar, S. (2021). "Increasing Warehouse Efficiency With Robotics," Robotics Tomorrow, August 3. www.roboticstomorrow.com/article/2021/07/increasing-warehouse-efficiency-with-robotics/17127.

Scheff, S. & Livingston D. (1991). Computer integrated logistics: CIL architecture in the extended enterprise. Southbury CT: IBM Corporation and U.S. Transportation Industry Marketing.

Stagl, A. J. (2021). "If the STB blesses its Pan Am marriage, CSX expects the union to be productive and fruitful," Progressive Railroad, October. www.progressiverailroad.com.

Stanley, L. (2014). *Effective Supply Management Performance* (2nd edn.). Tempe, AZ: Institute for Supply Management.

Stock, G., Greis, N., & Kasarda, D. (2000). "Enterprise logistics and supply chain structure: the role of fit," Journal of Operations Management, 18(5), 531–547.

Tai, M. C. (2020). "The impact of artificial intelligence on human society and bioethics," Tzu Chi Medial Journal 32(4), 339–343.

Toorajipou, R., Sohrabpour, V., Nazarpoir, A. Oghazi, P. and Fischi, M. (2021). "Artificial intelligence in supply chain management: A systematic literature review," Journal of Business Research (122) 502–517.

Transport Canada (2019). "Guideline for Remote Control Locomotive Operation." https://tc.canada.ca/en/rail-transportation/guidelines/guideline-remote-control-locomotive-operation.

Chapter 8

Sustainability in Transportation

Introduction

Environmental concerns came to the forefront of supply chain management in the 1980s and 1990s in response to the demand from governments to procure environmentally friendly products and services. As a result of this movement, a "cradle to grave" responsibility emerged, with entities making a commitment to be responsible for products throughout their lifecycle (Weiscott, 2000). Logistics management is at the heart of this movement, with organizations in all sectors considering issues such as recycling, remanufacturing, refurbishing, and disposal of packaging and products. Product categories that must be considered in the process include obsolete materials, scrap, and depleted equipment and products (Young, 2000). These initiatives ideally begin with the procurement process. Supply managers must determine factors involved in the total cost of ownership as it relates to logistics and incorporate them into their procurement strategies.

In more recent years, sustainability in the supply chain has evolved to include additional considerations. Along with environmental, there are the social and economic aspects of sustainability. Many refer to this concept as the *triple bottom line*, as it addresses profit, people, and planet in the strategy and operations of an organization (Mangan, et al, 2012).

DOI: 10.4324/9781003298625-8

Figure 8.1 Triple bottom line

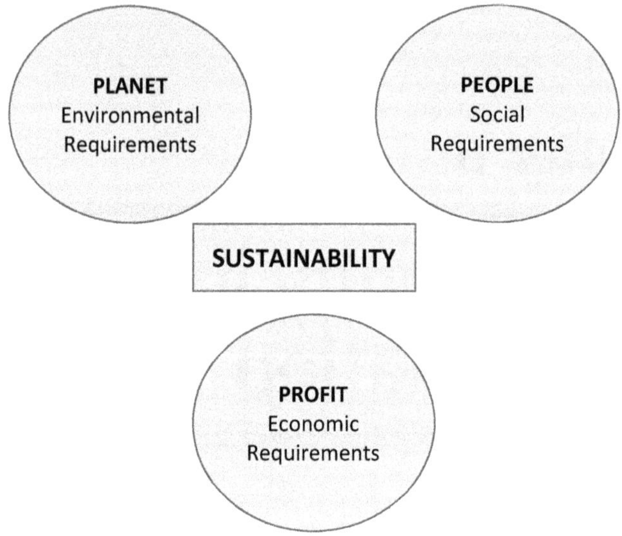

Reverse logistics

Environmental approaches include *green logistics* and *reverse logistics.* The term *green logistics* is used more broadly to describe "efforts to measure and minimize the environmental impact of logistics activities" (Rogers & Tibben-Lembke, 2001, p. 130). Reverse logistics is more specialized, focusing on the movement of material back from the point it was consumed to its original point. Stock (1998) defines *reverse logistics* as "the role of logistics in product return, source reduction, recycling, materials substitution, reuse of materials, waste disposal and refurbishing, repair, and remanufacturing" (p. 20). However, there is some overlap in the two terms, as pointed out by Rogers and Tibben-Lembke and shown in Figure 8.2.

Both reverse and green logistics cover recycling, remanufacturing, and the use of reusable packaging—for example, refillable bottles, reusable pallets, or reconditioned barrels. However, *green logistics* also refers to the reduction of packaging, air and noise emissions, and the environmental impact of mode selection.

There are many environmental issues that organizations face today. Industry leaders cite three major ones that supply chain professionals need to be aware of: global warming and climate change, water pollution, and loss of biodiversity. To best position the planet for future success, many believe

Figure 8.2 Reverse and green logistics activities

Material	*Reverse logistics activities*	*Overlap*	*Green logistics activities*
Products	Returns to supplier Resale Salvage Reconditioning Refurbishing Reclaiming Donation	Recycling Remanufacturing	Combined deliveries
Packaging	Refurbishing Reclaiming Salvage Landfill	Reusing Recycling	Reduction Sustainable packing

Source: Adapted from Schwartz, B. (2000). "Reverse logistics strengthens supply chains," Transportation and Distribution, 41(5); and Rogers, D. & Tibben-Lembke, R. (2001). "An examination of reverse logistics practices," Journal of Business Logistics, 22(2).

these three issues warrant immediate attention. With regard to global warming, organizations are encouraged to use more sustainable technology, work toward zero waste in commercial buildings, and improve waste compaction in landfills. Water pollution can be reduced by practicing more effective ways to contain spills, curtail stormwater runoff, and increase marine protection. Finally, to maintain balance in the ecosystem, government can implement better policies on conservation; more sustainable lifestyles can be adopted; and the general population can be better educated on biodiversity (Lawson, 2019).

It appears that leading organizations are better recognizing the priority that is placed on environmental standards by both consumers and producers. These include champions for environmental causes as well as policy leaders with a commitment to reverse logistics. This has motivated organizations in all sectors to implement better practices (Sarkis & Dou, 2018).

Recent Trends

A 2020 report from the EPA summarized trends in the generation of municipal solid waste (MSW). In an effort to report on the generation and disposition of waste in the United State, the EPA has collected data for more than 35 years. The information gathered can be used to measure the success of supply chain manager programs across the country (EPA, 2020).

The United States generated about 292 million tons of MSW in 2018, which is nearly double the amount generated in 1980 (151 million tons). On a positive note, recycling and composting programs are on the rise. Of the MSW generated in 2018, nearly 70 million tons were recycled and more than 25 million tons composted. This equates to a recycling and composting rate of just over 32% (EPA, 2020). Since the materials that are recycled or composted are considered to be diverted from a trip to the landfill, some organizations refer to this number as the *diversion rate.*

Results indicate that U.S. businesses today are doing a better job of materials and resource management. Pallets, for example, are being used multiple times before disposal rather than just once. Additionally, many organizations utilize composite pallets that are more durable and longer-lasting than traditional wood pallets. There have also been increased recycling efforts. However, Americans with more disposable income are creating more waste than the rest of the population. It is also estimated that the commercial sector accounts for approximately 40% of the waste generated in the United States. The commercial sector includes schools, government offices, hospitals, prisons, industrial sites, and businesses.

As recycling efforts increase in both the commercial and consumer sectors, the percentage of waste going into landfills is decreasing. In the past two decades this number has fallen from 57% to 50%. With improved material

Figure 8.3 Municipal solid waste generation, 1980–2018

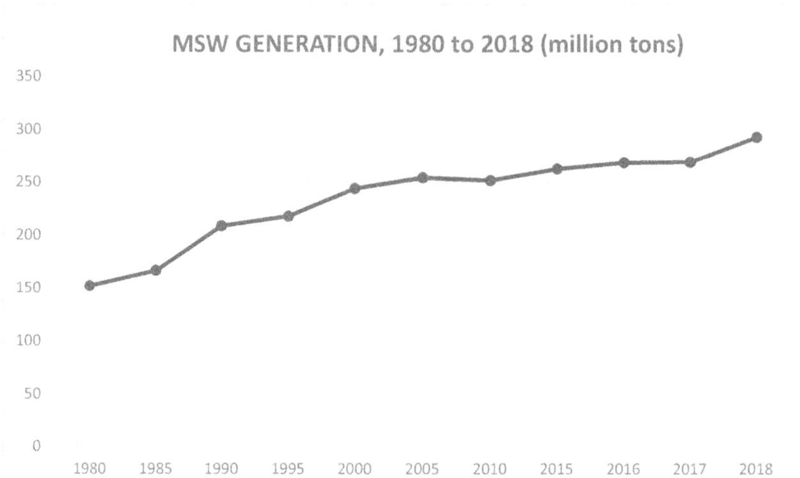

Source: Environmental Protection Agency (2020). Advancing Sustainable Materials Management: 2018 Fact Sheet Assessing Trends in Materials Generation and Management in the United States. www.epa.gov.

management practices, this percentage can continue to decrease, which will reduce the need for additional landfills. Containers and packaging, which play a significant role in logistics, continue to account for the highest rates of recycling. During 2018, containers and packaging were recycled at a rate of 54%.

The breakdown of landfilled materials can be seen in Figure 8.4. Food waste represents the largest portion of municipal solid waste, at 24.%. This is followed closely by plastics (18.5%), which many organizations continue to move away from using. While plastics have many uses and are durable, they are not recyclable.

The increase in online product ordering provides manufacturers and shippers an opportunity to reduce their environmental impact—for example, through consolidated shipments that reduce packaging, as well as the use of recycled and biodegradable shipping containers. An example of this is the Cainiao Network, the logistical arm of Alibaba Group, which reports that 100% of the packages shipped from its warehouses are biodegradable (Cainiao Network, 2020).

Other trends include the use of cleaner burning fuels in trucks and barges, as well as the use of delivery vehicles powered by electricity and compressed natural gas. UPS began offering bicycle delivery in Europe in 2012 and in 2016 it expanded this service to Portland, Oregon. This proved to be an ideal service model for a college campus, as Portland State University gladly partnered for success. In 2018, UPS expanded its program to e-bike delivery at the University of Washington in Seattle (Nickelsburg, 2018). Needless to say, this emission-free method of delivery works best in dense urban areas (Njus, 2016).

Figure 8.4 Landfilled materials

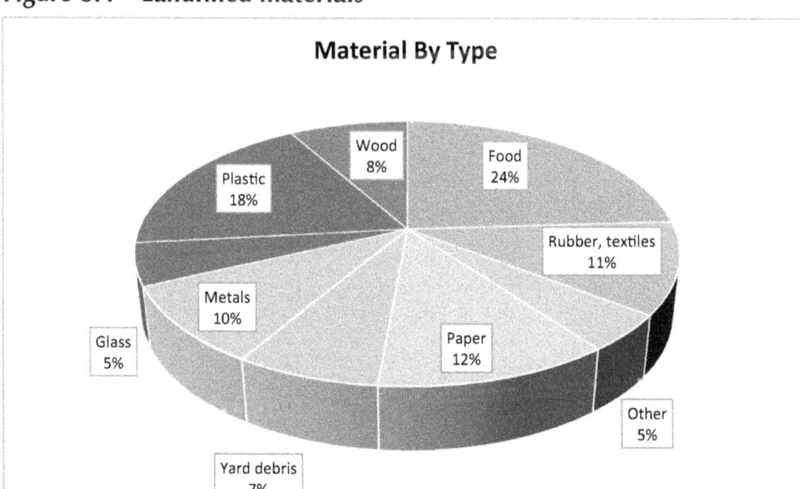

Total Cost of Ownership and Logistics Strategies

As entities move toward more sustainable practices, most have recognized that the total cost of an item goes beyond the initial buy to incorporate other activities, including final disposal—in other words, all costs tied to the lifecycle of the product. The *total cost of ownership* (TCO), a purchasing methodology, considers the cost of all activities attached to a particular product. *TCO* is defined as "the present value of all costs associated with a product, service, or capital equipment that are incurred over its expected life" (Menezes, 2001, p. 16). In addition to the actual purchase price, any costs related to the purchase and delivery of the product, use of the product, and disposition of the product when its useful life is over are part of the total cost of ownership. Ellram (1993) broke down the total cost of a product or service to include three categories of costs, as presented in Figure 8.5.

Environmental logistics activities come into play at all stages of the TCO analysis (Tibben-Lembke, 1998). An example of this is the EPA, which has developed various resources that help entities procure environmentally preferable products and services. Its guidance covers a wider range of commodities and products, and uses private sector approaches to define and measure sustainable product performance. The EPA program gives preference to multi-attribute/lifecycle-based standards that ensure product conformance by a bona fide third party (EPA, 2021).

In another case, a state issued an IFB in 2015 for fleet vehicles. The solicitation made it clear that TCO would be incorporated into the contract award criteria. The IFB used the formula set out in Figure 8.6 to determine the lowest cost to the state over the useful life of each vehicle. The contract award would

Figure 8.5 Total cost of ownership

Pre-transaction costs	Transaction costs	Post-transaction costs
Identify need	Determine price	Reject defects
Conduct RFQ	Place order	Field failures
Investigate sources	Manage delivery	Repair/replace in field
Qualify sources	Tariffs, duties	Customer goodwill
Add supplier	Billing and payment	Repair parts
Educate supplier	Inspection	Maintenance
Educate firm	Return of parts	Disposal and clean up
	Follow up and correction	Recycle, reuse

Source: Adapted from Ellram, L. (1993). "Total cost of ownership: Elements and implementation," International Journal of Purchasing and Materials Management. 29(4), 2–11; and Menezes, S. (2001). "Calculating the total cost of ownership," Purchasing Today (May), 16-17.

Figure 8.6 Contract award formula

$$CA = UP + G - R$$

UP	Unit price + weighted total adds – weighted total deducts
G	Projected fuel expenditure, adjusted to present value
R	Resale value, adjusted to present value

Source: Adapted from NIGP: The Institute for Public Procurement (2016). "Total Cost of Ownership: Realizing Procurement's Full Potential in Value Creation." www.nigp.org.

be based on the unit cost, expected fuel efficiency, and the resale value (NIGP, 2016).

Transaction costs can be positively affected if a supplier with a reverse or green logistics system can offer reconditioned or remanufactured products at a lower cost. For example, Massachusetts launched the Environmental Preferable Products Procurement Program to create demand for products that contain recyclable content and can be recycled. A list of sustainable products and services is maintained by the Operational Services Division of the Commonwealth. This includes contracts for green cleaners, biodiesel, and sustainable clothing (Commonwealth of Massachusetts, 2021).

Another consideration is the cost of a supplier offering to dispose of used products which, when passed along to the buying entity, increases transaction costs. The supplier's order placement and billing system is also important—that is, determining how quickly the entity will receive credit for returned goods so funds are freed up to purchase additional items.

If suppliers have integrated reverse logistics transportation with forward distribution costs, they may have improved buying power with their carriers, which can be passed on to the purchasing and supply management entity. Integration also improves transportation efficiencies because returned goods are carried on the backhaul.

Chrysler's plant in Belvidere, Illinois, relies upon employees to improve its practices in sustainability. Whether considering a backhaul or reducing waste/steps in the manufacturing process, this employee-owned operation continually seeks out ways to promote sustainability. In recent years, this has included the use of recycled water in liquid-cooled welders and a 219 metric ton reduction in CO_2 emissions by better organization of material deliveries (McGroarty, 2013).

The buying entity should determine the process for field failures. If the supplier has a reverse logistics system in place, instructions are generally provided for product return; therefore, convenience and satisfaction are improved. Products may also be repaired or remanufactured and returned to the client. *Repairing* is the process of making a product operational again, but a complete analysis may not necessarily be done and the product may not perform "as new." *Remanufacturing* means that a product has been completely disassembled and all parts have been examined for their condition, cleaned, repaired as necessary, tested, and reassembled to obtain optimal performance. The term *rebuilt* is used specifically in the automotive industry for vehicle parts. (More information is available at www.remanautomotiveparts.com/.) However, if the supplier does not have a reverse logistics system, the cost is borne as a separate expense by the buying entity. As a result, items will typically be stored until a sufficiently large shipment is justified. However, storage can result in damage or obsolescence, thus adding to the total cost of ownership.

The product will eventually reach the point of disposal. Regulatory compliance may dictate disposal, as in the case of products containing asbestos or lead. Total costs may be recouped to some extent if the product or parts are salvageable. Additionally, some manufacturers may take back the product for a fee and dispose of it properly. The Canadian government, for example, has created a comprehensive resource to help supply managers during the initial planning stages of a purchase to increase environmental responsibility. This includes the use of selection criteria that reduce greenhouse gas emissions and the use of sustainable plastics (Treasury Board of Canada, 2020).

Some issues that must be addressed regarding the disposal of products or their parts include the ability to:

- reuse or reallocate;
- resell to Canada's Crown Assets Distribution;
- return to the supplier for recycling, reuse, or recovery;
- recycle locally; or
- contribute to a waste exchange program.

Transportation and Location Issues

Transportation decisions are critical in recycling and reuse programs. Movement of used or recycled materials can be costly and can greatly reduce the financial benefits a program offers. Often, entities will choose the least expensive mode regardless of service levels. Rail is often chosen as the mode of choice over trucking strictly for cost reasons. Railroads move low-value commodities in high volumes at a low cost, with the added benefit of lower emissions of

CO_2 and nitrous oxide. Railroads also can accommodate container shipments, thus reducing the need for trucks.

More efficient use of trucks is another option. Using larger trucks for long-haul, direct transport results in fewer shipments and fewer emissions. Additionally, the hauling of two trailers by a single truck (double) results in reduced emissions. Domestic sea shipping is another less costly option that uses less fuel. Mitsubishi Electric of Japan, for example, moves a variety of products throughout its domestic market, including through sea and truck delivery methods. Its logistics center ships some 500 bicycles a day for Trek Japan, selecting the ideal mode of shipping to more than 300 stores across the country (Mitsubishi Electric, 2021).

A related consideration is the location for reverse logistics activities. Frequently, these sites are selected to minimize the costs of transportation. A centralized location may offer several benefits, including improved tracking of returns, customer satisfaction, safety, and time savings. Transportation companies and other third parties also may offer customized reverse logistics programs. In a 2019 report, Deloitte stressed the need for companies to develop a strategic approach to reverse logistics. The report notes a 33% increase in retail product returns, driven by a rise in e-commerce. Collaboration and coordination are the keys to employing a successful strategy that avoids a siloed approach to supply chain management (Deloitte, 2019).

Packaging and Movement of Hazardous Materials

A specialized form of environmental management practice is the packaging and movement of hazardous materials and waste. According to DOT, approximately 1.6 billion tons of hazardous materials are shipped annually in the United States (U.S. Department of Transportation, 2021). Shippers are considered to have an early but critical impact on the movement of hazardous materials.

Shippers play a key role in the safe transportation of hazardous materials to their destination. Caution should be exercised in selecting the carrier for the shipment of hazardous materials. Shippers must verify that the selected carrier has the appropriate licensing and experience to transport the particular type of hazardous material being shipped. In addition, the shipper must assure that the selected disposal site for the final destination of the material is licensed to store/dispose of that particular type of hazardous waste. The shipper must insist on receipt of a disposal certificate prior to releasing payment. Improper transportation or disposal of hazardous material may result in citations or penalties for the transporter or shipper.

As the generator of the hazardous material, the shipper may be responsible for that material regardless of any shipping arrangements or contracts. In cases where an entity lacks the resources to assure compliance with the many regulations on the transportation and disposal of hazardous waste, selecting a third-party logistics expert which can address all transportation and disposal issues may be the best solution for assuring compliance. Always investigate the capability of any third-party logistics handler through thorough reference verifications.

Multiple regulations govern the handling, packaging, and transportation of goods identified as hazardous materials. Several sections of the United States Code of Federal Regulations specific to the transportation, handling, and disposal of hazardous materials are found in Title 29, Title 40, and Title 49. Title 29 was created to protect the health and safety of employees that work with hazardous materials. The safe disposal of hazardous waste is covered under Title 40 and enforced by the EPA. Both the EPA and DOT have joint responsibility for the regulation of hazardous substances, defined as "severe pollutants to the environment" (United States Code Annotated, 1993, p.239). Title 49 is the statute regulating the transportation of hazardous materials and is jointly enforced by the Research and Special Programs Administration and DOT's individual agencies governing air, rail, highways, and the Coast Guard. Title 49 covers five areas, which are briefly described below.

Definition and Classification of Hazardous Materials

Several thousand of the most commonly transported hazardous materials are identified in the Hazardous Materials Table. They are divided into several classifications, including explosives, radioactive materials, gases, liquid and solid flammables, oxidizing materials, organic peroxides, corrosive materials, poisons, and miscellaneous. Some hazardous materials may be designated as "forbidden" and may not be transported at all. Other materials may not be transported by certain modes such as air transportation.

Communication and Labeling

Specific warning information must be communicated on shipping documents, package markings and labels, placards that appear on transportation vehicles and written emergency response information, including telephone numbers to be used in case of emergencies. Properly prepared shipping documents contain, at a minimum, an identification of the hazardous material and hazard class or division number, identification number, packing group, if applicable, and total quantity shipped.

Packaging Requirements

Markings and labels should contain similar information to that contained in the shipping documents. Information on the packaging should clearly identify that a package contains hazardous material. Any markings must be durable and readily visible. Title 49 includes specifications as to the size and color of warning labels.

Operations Rules

Operations rules include processes regarding incident reporting. For example, carriers must report all incidents, details of which are kept in an automated hazardous materials information system database. Any incidents involving aircraft shipments must be reported to the closest Civil Aviation Security Office of the FAA.

Training

All employees who perform functions in connection with hazardous materials must receive initial training and must update their training at least once every three years. If new regulations are adopted, employees must receive training on these requirements before they perform their functions again. The employer is responsible for providing the training and must keep records.

Regardless of an entity's size, several steps should be taken to manage the safe transportation of hazardous materials. The following should be considered when developing a training program (U.S. Department of Transportation):

- Develop and foster a culture of safety;
- Designate a training coordinator to lead the effort;
- Implement a strategic planning process for the training;
- Implement a consistent process for record keeping; and
- Develop a robust training curriculum.

Strategies for Successful Sustainability Programs

According to industry leaders, there are several things to consider in drawing up a step- by-step sustainability plan. More and more companies are pursuing sustainability programs because they believe this creates value for

Case Study: A Collaborative Effort in Sustainability

The University of California (UC) is comprised of 10 campuses throughout the state, along with a central administrative department in Oakland, the Office of the President. In 2018 a new policy was implemented that required the inclusion of sustainability in the selection criteria of all RFPs. A minimum of 15% of the available points in a solicitation would be attributed to the sustainable business practices of the responding supplier. This included all areas of sustainability (environmental, social, and economic) and applied to each RFP over $100,000, the formal solicitation threshold for the UC. While many were reluctant to embrace the new policy, they were soon dispelled when the Santa Cruz campus successfully awarded the first contract for its Silicon Valley Extension Program. The winning proposer was Pearson VUE, which scored well in the area of sustainability by highlighting its efforts in energy reduction, green travel, promoting women and minorities in the workplace, and offering a support program to employees during gender transition.

both them and their customers (Berg, 2015). Entities also need to consider why a plan is needed. There are multiple reasons, including compliance with regulatory statutes, protection of the environment, public opinion, and economic pressures. The EPA, for example, was authorized under Section 6002 of the Resource Conservation and Recovery Act and Executive Order 13101 to designate products made with recoverable materials and recommend practices to buy these products for all federal agencies (www.epa.gov/smm/comprehensive-procurement-guideline-cpg-program).

Once designated, that product must be procured with the highest practical recovered material content.

At this stage, entities also need to consider what resources they are willing to commit or can budget to implement an environmental program. A solid waste audit will help determine the types and volumes of solid waste generated. An audit should include the following steps:

- determining what is thrown away in dumpsters;
- visiting the landfill;
- interviewing employees; and
- identifying what waste is unique to your operation, such as supplier packaging.

The budget will determine the extent of the program. If faced with limited resources, the entity may want to consider hiring a third party or transportation company.

Once the idea has been accepted, how will the plan be communicated to end users or internal clients? Written instructions with preprinted labels from the manufacturer, emails, and newsletters are some of the more common ways to ensure compliance with the program. In some cases, additional training may be needed.

According to Sarkis and Dou (2018), sustainable supply chain strategies can be categorized in two ways: monitoring or collaboration. Sustainable strategies related to monitoring can include product eco-labeling, supplier compliance auditing, and supplier environmental questionnaires. Collaboration strategies include collaborating with suppliers on design, educating suppliers on sustainability policies, and influencing legislation related to sustainability. Figure 8.7 lays out some strategies to consider.

As an entity plans the process, it should develop a flowchart or process map, with detailed steps from origin of the returns process to final disposition of the waste/product. This flowchart or process map will provide a complete understanding of the internal operations and any shortcomings that could impede implementation. The map should include information about the following:

- Retrieval: Who will pick up the waste/product and how will this activity happen?
- Special training: This may be required of the transportation company and drivers, particularly for hazardous waste.
- Transportation: Be sure to provide accurate information, including weight, product classification, and a description on a bill of lading.

Figure 8.7 Sustainable supply chain strategies

Monitoring strategies	**Collaboration strategies**
• Product content requirements • Supplier environmental questionnaires • Product eco-labeling • Environmental management systems requirements • Supplier compliance	• Product stewardship • Supplier collaboration in design • Education suppliers • Joint development of green products • Influencing legislation in cooperation with suppliers

Source: Adapted from Sarkis, J. and Dou, Y. (2018). *Green Supply Chain Management.* New York: Routledge.

- Disposition: This entails handling returns in a centralized or regional location and determining how returns should be processed. Centralized locations allow for better data collection and tracking of returns to secondary markets overseas.

Develop an information system to support data collection and collect cost information. The Internet and cloud-based systems are frequently used as part of this system. Software should facilitate the backward movement of items smoothly and efficiently. Software that captures all details of the shipment and tracks shipment status should be integrated into the system. As with any software system, real-time data is the most useful.

Finally, know the financial and credit implications of the program. There may be refunds and credits from the manufacturer and inventory cost accounting issues. Once a plan has been developed, specific goals should be set, and a plan for education and training should be developed. All measurable, time-based goals should be tracked, followed by feedback and corrective action when necessary.

Conclusions

Entities have increased their efforts to be environmentally conscious and proactively pursue activities that involve reverse and sustainable logistics activities. Many state and local entities have implemented recycling and reuse programs to reduce pressure on landfills and improve conservation. TCO analysis, which measures the economic and environmental effects of a product through purchase, use, and disposal, is an important part of any sustainability program (National Center for Education Statistics, 2014). It is important to recognize that all supply chain members should be involved in sustainable activities.

The issue of practicing environmentally effective logistics has also resulted in entities outsourcing at least part of their reverse and green logistics functions. Third parties are increasingly meeting the needs of entities, often customizing their services to meet specific needs. Third parties may be particularly beneficial regarding transportation and disposal of hazardous waste. As a result, third parties have begun to form strategic alliances with other logistics providers to compile a complete package of services.

References

Berg, A. (2015). "Getting the most out of your sustainability program," McKinsey, August 1. www.mckinsey.com/industries/retail/our-insights/getting-the-most-out-of-your-sustainability-program.

Cainiao Network (2020). "Six Key Trends in Sustainable Logistics," December 3. https://cainiao.medium.com/6-key-trends-in-sustainable-logistics-55856e337ab7.
Commonwealth of Massachusetts (2021). "Environmentally Preferable Products Index," Operational Services Division. www.mass.gov/info-details/environmentally-preferable-products-index.
Currie, J. V. (1999). "Hazmat safety is no accident," Logistics Management and Distribution Report, 38(10).
Deloitte (2019). "Bringing it back: retailers need a synchronized reverse logistics strategy." www2.deloitte.com/us/en/pages/consulting/articles/reverse-logistics-management-for-supply-chains.html.
Ellram, L. (1993). "Total cost of ownership: Elements and implementation," International Journal of Purchasing and Materials Management, Fall, 2–11.
Fredette, M. (2001). "The benefits of green purchasing," Purchasing Today, April, 54–58.
Gooley, T. B. (1998). "Reverse logistics: Five steps to success," Logistics Management, June 49–54.
Kopicki, R. J., Berg, M. J., Legg, L. L., Dasappa, V., & Maggioni, C. (1993). *Reuse and Recycling Reverse Logistics Opportunities*. Oak Brook, IL: Council of Logistics Management.
Lawson, E. (2019). "Three environmental issues and ways to combat them," Environmental Protection, November 25. https://eponline.com/Articles/2019/11/25/Three-Environmental-Issues-and-Ways-to-Combat-Them.aspx?Page=1.
McGroarty, J. (2013). "How world-class manufacturing made one plant safer, greener, and more profitable," Plant Services, March 20. www.plantservices.com/articles/2013/04-plant-profile-chrysler-belvidere/
Menezes, S. (2001, May). "Calculating the total cost of ownership," Purchasing Today, 16–17.
Mitsubishi Electric (2021). "Logistics Corporation, Warehouse Management Services." www.mdlogis.co.jp/english/services/warehouse/.
Murphy, P. R., & Poist, R. F. (2000). "Green logistics strategies: An analysis of usage patterns," Transportation Journal, Winter 5–16.
National Center for Education Statistics (2014). "Total Cost of Ownership: An Important Piece of Any Sustainability Plan," April. https://nces.ed.gov/Programs/SLDS/pdf/TotalCostofOwnership.pdf
Nickelsburg, M. (2018). "UPS launches cargo e-bike delivery in Seattle, returning to bicycle courier origins a century later," Geekwire, October 26. www.geekwire.com/2018/ups-launches-cargo-e-bike-delivery-seattle-returning-bicycle-courier-origins-century-later/.
NIGP: The Institute for Public Procurement (2016). "Total Cost of Ownership: Realizing Procurement's Full Potential in Value Creation." www.nigp.org
Njus, E. (2016). "UPS debuts delivery by electric bike in Portland," The Oregonian, December 7. www.oregonlive.com
Programs Administration. (2000, March). *Departmentwide Program Evaluation of the Hazardous Materials Transportation Programs: Executive Summary*. Washington, DC: U.S. Department of Transportation.

Rogers, D., & Tibben-Lembke, R. (2001). "An examination of reversal logistics practices," Journal of Business Logistics, 22(2), 129–148.
Sarkis, J. & Dou, Y. (2018). *Green Supply Chain Management.* New York: Routledge.
Schwartz, B. (2000). "Reverse logistics strengthen supply chains," Transportation and Distribution, 41(5), 95–100.
Stock, J. R. (1998). *Development and Implementation of Reverse Logistics Programs.* Oak Brook, IL: Council of Logistics Management.
Tibben-Lembke, R. S. (1998). "The impact of reverse logistics on the total cost of ownership," Journal of Marketing Theory and Practice, 6(4), 51–60.
Treasury Board of Canada (2020). *Greening Government Strategy 2020.* www.canada.ca/en/treasury-board-secretariat/services/innovation/greening-government/strategy.html#toc3-5
United States Code Annotated. (1993). St. Paul, MN: West Publishing Company.
U.S. Department of Transportation (DOT). "Guide to Developing a Hazmat Training Program." www.phmsa.dot.gov/sites/phmsa.dot.gov/files/docs/training/hazmat/6586/guide-developing-hazmat-training-program.pdf
U.S. Environmental Protection Agency (EPA). (2021). *Recommendation of Specifications, Standards and Ecolabels for Federal Purchasing: 2021 Final Report.* Washington, DC: EPA:
U.S. Environmental Protection Agency (EPA). (2020, December). *Advancing Sustainable Materials Management: 2018 Fact Sheet.* Washington, DC: EPA
U.S. Environmental Protection Agency (EPA). (1999a, July). *Defending the Environment at the Department of Defense.* Washington, DC: EPA:
U.S. Environmental Protection Agency (EPA). (1999b). *Municipal Solid Waste in the United States: 1999 Final Report.* Washington, DC: EPA:
Weiskott, M. N. (2000). "Reverse logistics. Supply and Distribution." www.bizsites.com.
Young, R. R. (2000, July). "Supplier roles in environmental issues," *World Markets Series Business Briefing,* 59–64.

Index

www.ingramcontent.com/pod-product-compliance
Ingram Content Group UK Ltd.
Pitfield, Milton Keynes, MK11 3LW, UK
UKHW020135200926
475702UK00005B/762
* 9 7 8 1 0 3 2 2 8 8 1 1 6 *